THE HAMISH HAMILTON BOOK OF WISE ANIMALS

THE HAMISH HAMILTON BOOK OF

WISE ANIMALS

EDITED BY

EILÍS DILLON

ILLUSTRATED BY

BERNARD BRETT

HAMISH HAMILTON · LONDON

First published in Great Britain 1975
by Hamish Hamilton Children's Books Ltd
90 Great Russell Street, London WC1B 3PT

SBN 241 02156 1

Printed in Great Britain by
Western Printing Services Ltd, Bristol

Contents

Introduction

THE pleasure of living with animals comes to a great extent from watching how they make their needs and wishes known without using words. At most, a dog has a vocabulary of five words, a cat about the same, a horse perhaps four, a cow three. These are the animals we know best: no doubt if we lived in the jungle we should come to understand many more.

Once you begin to know the language, it is easy to see the wisdom and motives behind the animals' behaviour, and it is a short step from that to making up stories that fit in with their character and giving them human words to express themselves with. In this collection there are wise foxes, hares, pigs, dogs, cats and a cock. These nearly all appear in folk tales, made up by people who watched the animals around the house and farmyard. The other stories are imaginative, with animals behaving like people. These are allegorical, not to be really believed, but giving another dimension to what might have been just stories composed to show some aspect of the moral law. In fact they are works of art, with typical wavering outlines: is La Fontaine's ant really an ant, or is she a skinny, tight-lipped, self-satisfied spinster who keeps her own affairs in perfect order and cares nothing for what happens to her neighbours? That is how I have always seen her, and still she always managed to have an ant's face. But what does an ant's face look like? How should I know—unless it looks like a skinny, tight-lipped spinster as La Fontaine describes. Or does he?

So we go in and out of the animals' world with these stories and verses, wiser in the end and wishing we could get them to talk a little more. But if they did, it might not be half so much fun.

EILÍS DILLON

The Wolf and the Seven Little Kids

ONCE there was a mother goat and seven kids who lived all together in a little house on the edge of a forest. In the forest there lived a great fierce wolf who was always hungry. Now and then he passed by the little house and the mother goat and the kids could hear him say to himself:

"Aha! In there is a sweet little family, all ready for me to eat. One of these days I'll come and fetch them."

It happened that the mother goat had to go on a journey to a distant part of the forest, and before she set out she gathered the seven little kids together and said to them:

"Now, remember, while I'm out, do not on any account open the door. The wolf will be on the watch, and you may be sure he will try to come in while I'm gone and make away with you."

The kids shivered with excitement and said:

"How long will you be gone, Mama?"

"Three or four hours," said she. "And when I come back, I'll place my white hooves on the window-sill, where you can see them, so that you will know it is I. Then you can open the door and let me in."

Then she went off about her business, repeating her warning as she left and saying:

"Now remember, do not let anyone in, until I come and put my white hooves up on the window-sill."

The first hour passed quietly enough and then the little

kids heard the big greedy wolf come pounding and thrashing through the forest. As he approached the house, however, he became more discreet, and he walked up to the door as quietly as a rabbit.

He knocked three times, very gently.

"Who is there?" called out the eldest kid in a quavering voice.

"Your mother, returned from the other end of the forest," said the wolf.

The seven kids burst out laughing and the eldest said:

"We know you! You're the wolf! Our mother has a sweet, gentle voice and your voice is hoarse and growly."

There was no reply from outside the door and after a few minutes when they were sure he had quite gone, the seven little kids began to dance and sing around the kitchen:

"That's the way to get rid of the wolf!
That's the way to get rid of the wolf!
That's the way to get rid of the wolf—
And he won't come back again!"

But he did come back. Half an hour later, they heard him come quietly up to the door again and knock three times.

"Who is there?" called out the eldest kid, more bravely now.

"Your mother, returned from the other end of the forest," said the wolf in a sweet, gentle voice.

"That's our mother," said the second kid. "Let's open the door and let her in."

"No, no!" said the youngest. "That's the wolf, disguising his voice. If it's our mother, she will show her white hooves on the window-sill."

"Put your hooves up on the window-sill, where we can see them," the eldest kid called out.

Immediately the wolf sprang on his hind legs and placed his two great, hairy, grey, bristling forepaws on the window-sill. The seven kids burst out laughing and the eldest one said:

"We know you! You're the wolf! Our mother has beautiful white soft hooves and your paws are rough and grey and hairy."

There was no reply and after a while the seven little kids began to dance and sing around the kitchen:

"That's the way to get rid of the wolf!
That's the way to get rid of the wolf!
That's the way to get rid of the wolf—
And he won't come back again!"

But he did come back. Half an hour later, they heard him come quietly to the door and knock three times.

"Who is there?" called out the eldest kid, as bold as brass this time.

"Your mother, returned from the other end of the forest, and here are my beautiful white hooves to prove it," said the wolf in a sweet, gentle voice.

And he sprang up on his hind legs and placed two white hooves on the window-sill. He had gone off to the mill and dipped his two great, hairy, bristly, grey forepaws into the flour.

"It's our mother, all right," said the oldest kid.

"No, no," said the youngest. "That's the wolf."

"With those white hooves, and that gentle voice? How can you say it's the wolf when we know he has great hairy, bristly paws and a rough, growly voice? Let him in!"

So the oldest kid opened the door, and the wolf pranced

in, and swallowed up the first kid whole, and the second kid whole, and then the third, and the fourth and the fifth and the sixth. Then he began to look about for the youngest kid.

"That's funny," he said to himself, not bothering now to make his voice sweet and gentle. "Surely there were seven of them." Then he gave a great sleepy yawn and said: "Well, well, we must not be greedy. After a good meal, a little sleep."

And he lumbered off out of the house, leaving the door swinging open, and lay down on some dry leaves a short distance away, and went to sleep.

Presently the mother goat came back from her journey, and when she saw that the door of the house was standing open, she said to herself:

"The wolf has been here! How can they have been so foolish as to open the door to him?"

She went inside, and found not a single kid in sight, and she sat down on the floor and began to cry. At this the youngest kid, who was all the time hiding in the clock-case, called out:

"Mama! Mama! Here I am!"

And he climbed down and ran to tell her what had happened.

"So he came galloping in at the door, growling and howling, and I ran and hid in the clock-case, so here I am,' he said.

"But where are the others?"

"Inside the wolf," said the youngest kid. "He swallowed them whole."

"That's the first good news," said the mother goat briskly. "Where is he now?"

"Gone off to have a sleep on a pile of dry leaves."

So the mother goat took her needle and scissors and thread and went out into the forest, taking the youngest kid with her until they came upon the wolf fast asleep on his heap of leaves. She did not hesitate for a moment but cut him wide open, and out sprang the six kids. Then very quietly she brought six huge stones and put them inside him, and sewed him up neatly again, and they all went to wait at a little distance, for him to awaken. At last he did, in the late afternoon, yawning wide and saying to himself:

"After a good meal, a little sleep, after a little sleep, a long, cool drink."

And he set out for the deep pool in the forest, swaying from side to side because he was full of stones. The mother goat and the seven little kids followed him at a distance. At last, at the edge of the pool he bent down to drink, and at a signal from the mother goat they all got behind him and shoved and shoved and shoved until they shoved him right into the water, where he sank to the bottom.

Then the mother goat and the seven little kids began to dance and sing on the edge of the pool, and all the way home through the forest:

"That's the way to get rid of the wolf!
That's the way to get rid of the wolf!
That's the way to get rid of the wolf—
And he won't come back again!"

And this time, it was true.

Retold by EILÍS DILLON

Moreen

ONCE there was a very important gentleman who was married, and it was easy for him to be so because he had all the wealth in the world. He had a beautiful wife but after a while she was taken ill and in a very short time she died. There was great sorrow when this happened and she left only one child, a little girl named Moreen.

Now there was no one but Moreen and her father to see to their affairs, and since the girl was so young she was not able to do much. Her father was very fond of her, but after a while he married again and brought a stepmother in on top of poor Moreen.

Things went on, and the stepmother was very hard on her. She would not let her dress well and kept her most of the time in the ashes by the fire. Her father didn't know how hard things were with Moreen, and when the stepmother had a daughter of her own, she made life even worse for Moreen and would have liked to do away with her altogether, but she didn't dare to suggest it, because Moreen's father was so fond of her. The stepmother was so cruel that when her own daughter grew up she made Moreen do all the housework, and never had her own daughter do a hand's turn.

When Moreen was older, she found out where her mother was buried and then she used to go to the graveyard every day and spend a long time there crying. There were many bones around the grave, and she gathered up the bones and put them in her apron, and there she would sit crying, holding the bones in her apron.

One day she was like this, crying and with her apron full of bones, but when she opened out the apron, instead of the bones she found a lovely little black cat. She was very frightened, but the cat spoke to her saying:

"Don't be afraid. You have a wicked stepmother but you'll get the better of her yet, because I'll always be with you to help you. Nothing will happen to you that I won't know about and I'll be at hand whenever you want me."

This was fair enough and she went home, and endured the same ill-treatment from her stepmother and her step-sister. After a while, the stepmother decided to do away with her altogether, and one day she told Moreen that they would all go for an outing and a walk to a certain place. Moreen went with her, and where did the stepmother go but into a deep wood. The wood had a bad name, because it was said that some robbers lived there, and sure enough as they were going along, the robbers leaped out on them and demanded money from them.

"I have as much money as you want," said the step-mother, "but you must do something for me in return."

"What must we do?" asked the robbers.

"You must take away this girl and kill her!"

"We'll do that for you," they said. "Just give us the money."

She gave them lots of money, and handed over Moreen to them, and then she went home.

So things remained but after a few days the father noticed that Moreen was not to be seen about the place. He asked the stepmother where she was but she said she didn't know, that Moreen had probably gone off somewhere and would be back in a few days.

The father did no more about it. Meanwhile the robbers had Moreen with them, and though they had been paid a lot of money they were not so wicked as to kill such a lovely girl.

"Don't be afraid," they said to her. "We won't kill you —but we don't want to send you back to that woman either."

Moreed told them that it was her stepmother and that she had always treated her very badly. The robbers were very sorry for her and took her through the wood to a place where there was a little old house. They locked her in, saying:

"Stay here. There is no fear you will die, because we will bring you food now and then."

Then they went off and left her.

Moreen began to cry when she realised what had happened to her, but soon the little black cat came and spoke to her:

"Don't be afraid, though your stepmother has played a dirty trick on you. She will not succeed. You should be thankful to the men who put you in here, since they might have killed you as they had been paid to do by your stepmother. She is the one you must keep clear of. You'll find you won't go hungry."

So Moreen stayed in the little old house. That cat came to her very often and brought her food too, so that she wanted for nothing.

When she had been a few years in the hut, one day there was to be a big fair in the district, and the black cat came to her the same day and said:

"Get ready to go to the fair."

"How can I get ready—I have nothing to wear."

"I'll get you ready, then," said the cat. "Come outside with me."

Moreen followed her outside and the cat said:

"Now take this rush in your hand and pull it."

Moreen did as she was told and the rush became the most beautiful dress that a woman had ever worn, the colour of white silver.

"Now pull this other rush," said the cat

When Moreen did so, it became the smartest little pony that ever was seen.

"Put on the dress," said the cat, and when she put it on she looked very beautiful.

"Now mount your horse, go to the fair and ride all around it. Don't speak to anyone, and when you have ridden all around the fair several times, come back to me here."

She went to the fair and everyone there gazed at her beautiful dress and her fine horse, as well as at the beauty of the girl herself.

At the fair there was a nobleman who took a great interest in this fair always, and he was riding around looking at everything. He noticed the girl with the beautiful dress but she made sure to avoid him until she left the fair. She came home and told the black cat what had happened.

"Yes, you did very well," said the cat, "but there is still something that you must do."

The nobleman lived near the fair, and when he got home he could not stop talking about the lovely girl he had seen, with the beautiful dress and the fine horse. Indeed everyone in the whole district was talking about the woman who had been seen at the fair.

On the second day of the fair, the black cat said to Moreen:

"You must go again."

"What must I do this time?" she asked.

"You must do the same again," said the cat. "Come with me outside." When they were outside the cat said: "Take this rush in your hand and pull it." She did so, and as soon as she pulled on the rush it became a beautiful dress again, this time the colour of gold. "Now pull the rush next to it," said the cat. When she did so, it became a fine horse, of a different colour from the day before.

"Mount the horse," said the cat ,"and go to the fair, and the nobleman will watch you even more closely than he did yesterday, and perhaps he will try to speak to you, if he sees an opportunity. But you must not speak to him but leave the fair as soon as you have ridden around it several times."

Off she went and into the field where the fair was going on. Everyone was gazing at her, and there was no one there who could come near her for elegance and beauty. You may be sure that the nobleman was watching her but she kept well away from him. He moved towards the gateway so as to be there before her and speak to her but she swept past him on the horse without stopping, so that he was more distressed than ever that she had got away from him.

Moreen went home and told the black cat what had happened.

"Good enough," said the cat. "Everything will be all right yet."

Before long, the nobleman arranged to have another fair, in the hope that she would come and that he would see her again. Moreen's stepsister wanted to marry him, and she had great hopes of him because she too was a beautiful girl. She put on the best dress she could get and harnessed her best horse, but she could not come near the dress nor the horse that Moreen had.

On the morning of the fair, the black cat came and told Moreen that she must go, and this she was willing to do.

"Come outside with me, then," said the cat. They went outside and the cat showed her a rush. "Pull on this," she said and as soon as Moreen did, it became the most beautiful dress in the world, much more beautiful than any she had worn before. It was the colour of a rainbow. "Pull another rush," said the cat, and when she did, it became a fine horse.

"Now," said the cat, "mount your horse and take a turn around the fair as you did before."

She did so, and never stopped until she was in the midst of the fair. The nobleman was there, watching out to see if she would come. Then he saw a girl on a horse, wearing a beautiful dress. This was Moreen's stepsister, and he went to speak to her, but while they were together, who should pass by but Moreen on her way out of the fair. The nobleman recognised her at once and whipped up his horse, to reach the gate before her. He reached it, and made a grab at the horse's bridle to stop it. He did not succeed, but he managed to seize one of Moreen's shoes and keep it, so that she had to gallop home to the black cat with only one shoe.

"Where did you lose the other shoe?" asked the cat. Moreen described what had happened and the cat said: "Perhaps that is for the best."

The stepsister rode home and consulted her magic mirror, as she was accustomed to once a year. Gazing into it she said:

"Mirror of magic hanging there,
Of all the world's women, am I now the most fair?"

The mirror gave her this answer:

"You're fair enough, such as you are,
But the girl called Mor is fairer by far."

When they heard that Mor was alive, the stepsister and stepmother turned black and blue with rage. They thought she had been killed long ago by the robbers.

They went at once to visit an old wizard that they knew, to ask him about Moreen and find out whether she was alive or dead.

"I know very well that she is alive," said he.

"And where is she?" asked the stepmother.

"She is in a certain wood," said he, "in a little hut there, all alone, and she has been there for a long time."

"Very well," said the stepmother, "we must consider and work out another trick to play on her."

They sent their servants to the wood to look for Moreen, and she was found and brought back to the stepmother. Her father welcomed her home, astonished that she should have stayed away so long. Moreen told him nothing of where she had been.

Soon the nobleman made an announcement that he would go from house to house all over the whole district, looking for the girl that the shoe would fit, and that if he could not find her he would never marry at all. He set out on this mission, but he failed to find any girl who could put on the shoe.

At last he came to the house where Moreen was. The stepmother and her daughter were ready for him, and the daughter had spent a long time in preparing to force the shoe on to her foot, almost to the point of cutting off her toes or taking slices off her heels, for they knew it was a very small shoe. When the nobleman was coming near, they set upon Moreen and hid her under a big cupboard.

The nobleman came in and said:

"I wonder if this shoe will fit any of you?"

"It probably will," said the stepsister.

He handed her the shoe and she did her best to get it on to her foot, but she failed completely. At that moment a little black cat walked in, leaped on to the cupboard and said:

"Moreen, Moreen, hidden from you,
Could easily put her foot in that shoe."

"Chase that old devil of a cat out of there!" said the mother.

They chased her, but she hung around by the door while the mother was trying on the shoe herself. Then she leaped on to the cupboard again and said:

"Moreen, Moreen, hidden from you,
Could easily put her foot in that shoe."

"Chase away that terrible cat," said the old woman again, and this was done, but she came back and said the same thing a third time.

"Why can't you keep that cat out of the house?" the old woman said to her daughter, but the nobleman said:

"I want to know what is in that cupboard. The cat seems to know what she's saying."

He opened the cupboard, and there was Moreen inside.

"Come out," said he.

"I'd like to," she said, "but I was put in here by my stepmother and stepsister."

"Come out anyway," said he. "I have a shoe here, and who knows but it may fit you?"

She came out, and picked up the shoe and put it on, and anyone could see at once that it was made for her.

"That is your shoe," said he, "and you are my wife!"

He took her by the hand and led her out of the house, leaving the stepmother and stepsister behind. He took her to his home and not long afterwards they were married.

After a while Moreen had a son. Then her stepsister came to ask about her.

"You have been a long time in coming," said the nobleman.

"That is so," said she, "but after all, she is my sister, and no matter how it is between us, quarrels between friends never last long."

But she gave some money to the midwife, asking her to give her the child and to say that it was dead. The midwife did this—money is a powerful way to soften people. The stepsister took the child away with her.

The nobleman's house was on the coast, and a great cliff overhung the sea there. She took the child and threw it over the cliff, down into the sea. The nobleman believed the story of the old midwife that the child had died and was buried, and that there was nothing more to be said or done about it.

Then Moreen had another son, and again her stepsister came to visit her and played the same trick on her. She bribed the midwife to give her the child and did the same as she had done before. She wanted to turn the nobleman against Moreen, so that she could have him for herself.

Again Moreen had a son, and again the stepsister came, bribed the old midwife, took the child and threw it over the cliff as she had done with the other two. Then she went away, but soon she was back for a visit to Moreen, saying:

"I have come to visit you so that we may become real friends, and I am going to stay with you for a week."

This she did, and after a few days she said to Moreen:

"It's bad for your health to mope all day in the house. You should come out and take a walk with me."

She persuaded Moreen to go for a walk with her, along the top of the cliff, but when they were at the highest part, suddenly she caught her by the arm and the leg and threw her over the cliff into the sea.

She went running back to the house, pretending to be panting, and told the nobleman what had happened to Moreen, that she had fallen over the cliff into the sea. A search party went out to look for her but no trace of Moreen could be found.

After a while, since Moreen was gone, the nobleman thought of marrying again, and whom should he choose but the stepsister. Indeed he thought that this would be the right thing to do. He did marry her but though he thought it was right, he never liked her.

A good while after they were married, a servant boy of theirs was walking on the cliff above the sea when he looked down on to the beach below and saw a woman away down there, with one child at her breast and two playing around with a black cat on the sand beside her. He was astonished, and when he came home he told the nobleman what he had seen. But the nobleman took no notice of him: he did not believe him at all. A few days later, the servant boy saw them again, and this time he said to the nobleman that the woman he had seen was very like Moreen.

At this the nobleman took some notice of him.

"The next time you go near the cliff, make sure that I am with you," he said.

Soon afterwards he called the servant boy and said that they would go to the cliff together, to see the woman and the children. They walked on the cliff-top and sure enough very soon they saw the woman and the children and the little black cat, as the servant boy had said. The nobleman climbed down the face of the cliff, slipping and sliding, from one foothold to another, until he was near enough to seize hold of the woman, and who should it be but Moreen.

"So this is where you are!" he said. "We searched everywhere for you when you fell over the cliff."

"I was thrown over the cliff," said she, "and here I have been since. It's not a bad life. I have a little house in the face of the cliff, and the little black cat makes sure that neither I nor the three children want for anything."

"And who are the three children?" asked the nobleman.

"My own three sons," said she, "and your three sons. These are the three children I had, and the woman you have since married, my own stepsister, bribed the midwife, and got the children from her, and threw them over the cliff. But the black cat saved them and we have been here ever since."

"Thats' enough," said the nobleman. "Now you can all come home."

"Yes," she said. "There is no reason why we should not."

He took her home with him, as well as the three children—two of them were well-grown boys—and he sent for his wife at home, who was Moreen's stepsister. He asked her if the story was true and she tried to deny it, but she could not. Moreen told exactly what had happened, and then the midwife was sent for. She came, and admitted that she had taken a bribe from the woman that the nobleman had married, Moreen's stepsister.

"Very well," said the nobleman. "She will bribe you no more. I will not do you any harm, though you have deserved it as much as she has."

Then he took the woman out to the top of the cliff. He threw her over and went home. After that she was never seen again, alive or dead.

Word went to the mother that her daughter had fallen over the cliff and had not been found. The mother came and asked the nobleman and Moreen to go with her to the cliff-top, and show her the place where her daughter had fallen. They went, and while she was looking down from the place where the stepsister had fallen, Moreen pushed her over the cliff, and neither she nor the nobleman stayed to give as much as one look, to see what became of her. The old woman was drowned, and probably a whale or some other monster has eaten her up long since—herself and that wicked daughter of hers.

From that day onwards the black cat was not seen, and the nobleman asked Moreen to tell about her. She told him the whole story from beginning to end, how she used to pray and weep on her mother's grave, and how the black cat first came to her there, and how it did so much for her, and Moreen said that the black cat was surely her own mother who had put on this form so that she could come to her.

"It was the same black cat that was on top of the cupboard," she said, "on the day that you came to us with the shoe. But now that cat does not come at all, because from now on we have no need of it. From now on we can live happily, because there is an end to my stepmother and my stepsister."

Translated from an Irish Folk-tale by EILÍS DILLON

The Psammead

E. NESBIT

Edith Nesbit's story Five Children and It *is about a family on holiday in Kent. They go to play in an old sandpit and one of them digs up a sand-fairy that has been lying asleep there for thousands of years. This is the Psammead, which soon tells them that they can have a wish every day. . . .*

THE cave was disappointing, because there were no shells, and the wrecked ship's anchor turned out to be only the broken end of a pickaxe handle, and the cave party were just making up their minds that sand makes you thirstier when it is not by the seaside, and someone had suggested going home for lemonade, when Anthea suddenly screamed:

"Cyril! Come here! Oh, come quick! It's alive! It'll get away! Quick!"

They all hurried back.

"It's a rat, I shouldn't wonder," said Robert. "Father says they infest old places—and this must be pretty old if the sea was in here thousands of years ago."

"Perhaps it's a snake," said Jane, shuddering.

"Let's look," said Cyril, jumping into the hole. "I'm not afraid of snakes. I like them. If it is a snake I'll tame it, and it will follow me everywhere and I'll let it sleep around my neck at night."

"No, you won't," said Robert firmly. He shared Cyril's bedroom. "But you may if it's a rat."

"Oh, don't be silly," said Anthea; "it's not a rat, it's *much* bigger. And it's not a snake. It's got feet; I saw them; and fur! No—not the spade. You'll hurt it! Dig with your hands."

"And let *it* hurt *me* instead! That's so likely, isn't it?" said Cyril, seizing the spade.

"Oh, don't!" said Anthea. "Squirrel, *don't*. I—it sounds silly but it said something. It really and truly did."

"What?"

"It said, 'You let me alone.' "

But Cyril merely observed that his sister must have gone off her nut, and he and Robert dug with spades while Anthea sat on the edge of the hole, jumping up and down with hotness and anxiety. They dug carefully and presently everyone could see that there really was something moving at the bottom of the Australian hole.

Then Anthea cried out, "I'm not afraid. Let me dig," and fell on her knees and began to scratch like a dog does when he has suddenly remembered where it was that he buried his bone.

"Oh, I felt fur," she cried, half laughing and half crying. "I did indeed. I did!" when suddenly a dry, husky voice in the sand made them all jump back, and their hearts jumped nearly as fast as they did.

"Let me alone!" it said.

And now every one heard the voice and looked at the others to see if they had too.

"But we want to see you," said Robert bravely.

"I wish you'd come out," said Anthea, also taking courage.

"Oh, well—if that's your wish," the voice said, and the sand stirred and spun and scattered, and something brown and furry and fat came rolling out of the hole, and the sand fell off it, and it sat there yawning, and rubbing the ends of its eyes with its hands.

"I believe I must have dropped asleep," it said, stretching itself.

The children stood round the hole in a ring, looking at the creature they had found. It was worth looking at. Its eyes were on long horns like a snail's eyes, and it could move them in and out like telescopes; it had ears like a bat's ears, and its tubby body was shaped like a spider's and covered with thick fur; its legs and arms were furry too, and it had hands and feet like a monkey's.

"What on earth is it?" Jane said. "Shall we take it home?"

The thing turned its long eyes to look at her and said:

"Does she always talk nonsense, or is it only the rubbish on her head that makes her silly?"

It looked scornfully at Jane's hat as it spoke.

"She doesn't mean to be silly," Anthea said gently; "we none of us do, whatever you may think! Don't be frightened; we don't want to hurt you, you know."

"Hurt *me! Me* frightened? Upon my word! Why, you talk as if I were nobody in particular."

All its fur stood out like a cat's when it is going to fight.

"Well," said Anthea, still kindly, "perhaps if we knew who you are in particular we could think of something to say that wouldn't make you cross. Everything we've said so far seems to have. Who are you? And don't get angry! Because really we don't know."

"You don't know?" it said. "Well, I knew the world had changed—but—well, really—do you mean to tell me seriously you don't know a Psammead when you see one?"

"A Sammyadd? That's Greek to me."

"So it is to everyone," said the creature sharply. "Well,

in plain English, then, a *Sand-fairy*. Don't you know a Sand-fairy when you see one?"

It looked so grieved and hurt that Jane hastened to say:

"Of course I see you are *now*. It's quite plain now one comes to look at you."

"You came to look at me, several sentences ago," it said crossly, beginning to curl up again in the sand.

"Oh—don't go away again! Do talk some more." Robert cried. "I didn't know you were a Sand-fairy, but I knew directly I saw you that you were much the wonderfullest thing I'd ever seen."

The Sand-fairy seemed a shade less disagreeable after this.

"It isn't talking I mind," it said, "as long as you're reasonable civil. But I'm not going to make polite conversation for you. If you talk nicely to me, perhaps I'll answer you, and perhaps I won't. Now say something."

Of course no one could think of anything to say, but at last Robert thought of, "How long have you lived here?" and he said it at once.

"Oh, ages—several thousand years," replied the Psammead.

"Tell us all about it. Do."

"It's all in books."

"*You* aren't," Jane said. "Oh, tell us everything you can about yourself! We don't know anything about you, and you *are* so nice."

The Sand-fairy smoothed his long rat-like whiskers and smiled between them.

"Do please tell!" said the children all together.

It is wonderful how quickly you get used to things, even the most astonishing. Five minutes before, the children had had no more idea than you that there was such a thing as a sand-fairy in the world, and now they were talking to it as if they had known it all their lives.

It drew its eyes in and said:

"How very sunny it is—quite like old times. Where do you get your Megatheriums from now?"

"What?" said the children all at once. It is very difficult to remember that "what" is not polite, especially in moments of surprise or agitation.

"Are Pterodactyls plentiful now?" the Sand-fairy went on.

The children were unable to reply.

"What do you have for breakfast?" the Fairy said impatiently, "and who gives it to you?"

"Eggs and bacon, and bread-and-milk, and porridge and things. Mother gives it to us. What are Mega-what's-its-names and Ptero-what-do-you-call-thems? And does anyone have them for breakfast?"

"Why, almost everyone had Pterodactyl for breakfast in my time! Pterodactyls were something like crocodiles and something like birds—I believe they were very good grilled. You see it was like this: of course there were heaps of sand-fairies then, and in the morning early you went out and hunted for them, when you'd found one, it gave you your wish. People used to send their little boys down to the seashore early in the morning before breakfast to get the day's wishes, and very often the eldest boy in the family would be told to wish for a Megatherium, ready jointed for cooking. It was as big as an elephant, you see, so there was a good deal of meat on it. And if they wanted fish, the Ichthyosaurus was asked for—he was twenty to forty feet long, so there was plenty on him. And for poultry there was Plesiosaurus; there were nice pickings on that too. Then the other children could wish for other

things. But when people had dinner-parties it was nearly always Megatheriums; and Ichthyosaurus, because his fins were a great delicacy and his tail made soup."

"There must have been heaps and heaps of cold meat left over," said Anthea, who meant to be a good housekeeper some day.

"Oh, no," said the Psammead, "that would never have done. Why, of course, at sunset what was left over turned into stone. You find the stone bones of the Megatherium and things all over the place even now, they tell me."

"Who tell you?" asked Cyril; but the Sand-fairy frowned and began to dig very fast with its furry hands.

"Oh, don't go!" they all cried; "tell us more about it when it was Megatheriums for breakfast. Was the world like this then?"

It stopped digging.

"Not a bit," it said; "it was nearly all sand where I lived, and coal grew on trees, and the periwinkles were as big as tea-trays—you find them now; they're turned into stone. We sand-fairies used to live on the seashore, and the children used to come with their little flint-spades and flint-pails and make castles for us to live in. That's thousands of years ago, but I hear that children still build castles on the sand. It's difficult to break yourself of a habit."

"But why did you stop living in the castles?" asked Robert.

"It's a sad story," said the Psammead gloomily. "It was because they *would* build moats to the castles, and the nasty wet bubbling sea used to come in, and of course as soon as a sand-fairy got wet it caught cold, and generally died. And so there got to be fewer and fewer, and whenever you found a fairy and had a wish, you used to wish for a Megatherium, and eat twice as much as you wanted, because it might be weeks before you got another wish."

"And did *you* get wet?" Robert inquired.

The Sand-fairy shuddered.

"Only once," it said; "the end of the twelfth hair of my top left whisker—I feel the place still in damp weather. It was only once, but it was quite enough for me. I went away as soon as the sun had dried my poor dear whisker. I scurried away to the back of the beach, and dug myself a house deep in warm dry sand, and there I've been ever since. And the sea changed its lodgings afterwards. And now I'm not going to tell you another thing."

"Just one more, please," said the children. "Can you give wishes now?"

"Of course," it said; "didn't I give you yours a few minutes ago? You said, 'I wish you'd come out,' and I did."

Oh, please, mayn't we have another?"

"Yes, but be quick about it. I'm tired of you."

I daresay you have often thought what you would do if you had three wishes given you, and have despised the old man and his wife in the black-pudding story, and felt certain that if you had the chance you could think of three really useful wishes without a moment's hesitation. These children had often talked this matter over but, now the chance had suddenly come to them, they could not make up their minds.

"Quick," said the Sand-fairy crossly. No one could think of anything, only Anthea did manage to remember a private wish of her own and Jane's which they had never told to the boys. She knew the boys would not care about it—but still it was better than nothing.

"I wish we were all as beautiful as the day," she said in a great hurry.

The children looked at each other, but each could see that the others were not any better-looking than usual. The Psammead pushed out its long eyes, and seemed to be holding its breath and swelling itself out till it was twice as fat and furry as before. Suddenly it let its breath go in a long sigh.

"I'm really afraid I can't manage it," it said apologetically. "I must be out of practice."

The children were horribly disappointed.

"Oh, *do* try again!" they said.

"Well," said the Sand-fairy, "the fact is, I was keeping back a little strength to give the rest of you your wishes with. If you'll be contented with a wish a day amongst the lot of you I daresay I can screw myself up to it. Do you agree to that?"

"Yes, oh, yes!" said Jane and Anthea. The boys nodded. They did not believe the sand-fairy could do it. You can always make girls believe things much easier than you can boys.

It stretched out its eyes farther than ever, and swelled and swelled and swelled.

"I do hope it won't hurt itself," said Anthea.

"Or crack its skin," Robert said anxiously.

Everyone was very much relieved when the Sand-fairy, after getting so big that it almost filled up the hole in the sand, suddenly let out its breath and went back to its proper size.

"That's all right," it said, panting heavily. "It'll come easier to-morrow."

"Did it hurt much?" asked Anthea.

"Only my poor whisker, thank you," said he, "but you're a kind and thoughtful child. Good day."

It scratched suddenly and fiercely with its hands and

feet, and disappeared in the sand. Then the children looked at each other, and each child suddenly found itself alone with three perfect strangers, all radiantly beautiful.

So they are as beautiful as the day, but the Psammead forgot to mention that every single wish they were given would turn out to be such a nuisance that they would have been far better off without it.

From FIVE CHILDREN AND IT

The Three Little Pigs

ONCE upon a time three little Pigs, not very old nor very wise, were left alone in the world by reason of the death of their mother, who was taken from them by a greedy butcher. The little Pigs did not always agree so well together as was right, and it was not long before they decided to set up housekeeping independently, instead of sharing the home where they had been brought up. Each thought he knew best how to build himself a house, and how to look after himself. So they parted, and set off in different ways to seek their fortune.

The first little Pig had not gone far before he met a Man with a bundle of straw.

"Please, Man, give me that straw to build a house," said he.

The Man gave him the straw, and the little Pig built a house with it. Presently a Wolf came along, and knocked at the door and said:

"Little Pig, little Pig, let me come in."

But the little Pig knew it was the Wolf, and answered:

"No, no, by the hair on my chinny chin chin!"

"What!" said the Wolf. "Then I'll huff, and I'll puff, and I'll blow your house in."

So he huffed, and he puffed, and he blew the house in, and ate up the first little Pig.

The second little Pig met a Man with a bundle of furze, and said:

"Please, Man, give me that furze to build a house."

The Man gave him the furze, and the little Pig built his house. Then along came the Wolf, and knocked at the door, and said:

"Little Pig, little Pig, let me come in."

But the little Pig knew him and answered:

"No, no, by the hair on my chinny chin chin!"

"Then I'll huff, and I'll puff, and I'll blow your house in."

So he huffed, and he puffed, and he puffed, and he huffed, and he blew the house in, and ate up the second little Pig.

The third little Pig met a Man with a load of bricks and said:

"Please, Man, give me those bricks to build a house with."

The Man gave him the bricks and he built a house with them. Presently the Wolf came by, as he did to the other little Pigs, and said: "Little Pig, little Pig, let me come in."

"No, no, by the hair on my chinny chin chin!"

"Then I'll huff and I'll puff, and I'll blow your house in."

Well, he huffed and he puffed, and he huffed and he puffed, and he puffed and huffed, but he could not blow the house in. When he found that he could not, with all his huffing and puffing, blow the house in, he said:

"Little Pig, I know where there is a nice field of turnips."

"Where?" said the little Pig.

"Oh, in Farmer Smith's field, and if you will be ready to-morrow morning early, I will call for you, and we will go together and get some for dinner."

"Very well," said the little Pig; "I will be ready. What time do you mean to go?"

"Oh, at six o'clock."

Well, the little Pig got up at five, and got the turnips before the Wolf came, which he did about six.

"Little Pig, are you ready?" said the Wolf when he arrived.

"Ready!" said the little Pig. "I have been and come back again, and got a nice potful for dinner."

The Wolf felt very angry at this, but thought that he would be even with the little Pig somehow or other, so he said:

"Little Pig, I know where there is a nice apple-tree."

"Where?" said the Pig.

"In the orchard near the village," replied the Wolf, "and if you will not deceive me, I will come for you at five o'clock to-morrow and get some apples."

Well, the little Pig bustled up the next morning at four o'clock, and went off for the apples, hoping to get back before the Wolf came; but he had farther to go than the day before, and had to climb the tree, so that just as he was coming down from it, he saw the Wolf coming, which frightened him very much. When the Wolf came up, he said:

"Little Pig, what! Are you here before me? Are they nice apples?"

"Yes, very," said the little Pig. "I will throw you down one."

He threw down one, and threw it so far that, while the Wolf was gone to pick it up, the little Pig climbed down quickly and ran home and shut himself in.

The next day the Wolf came again, and said to the little Pig:

"Little Pig, there is a fair in the village this afternoon. Will you go?"

"Yes," said the little Pig. "I will go; what time will you be ready?"

"At three," said the Wolf.

But the little Pig went off before the time again, and got to the fair, and bought a butter-churn, which he was going home with when he saw the Wolf coming. Then he could not tell what to do. So he got into the churn to hide, and by so doing turned it round, and it rolled down the hill with the Pig in it, making such a strange noise that it frightened the Wolf very much, so much that he ran home without going to the fair. He went to the little Pig's house, and told him how frightened he had been by a great round thing which came down the hill past him.

Then the little Pig said:

"Hah! I frightened you, then. I had been to the fair and bought a butter-churn, and when I saw you, I got into it, and rolled down the hill."

Then the Wolf was very angry indeed, and declared he would eat up the little Pig and that he would come down the chimney after him. When the little Pig saw what he was about, he hung the pot full of water over the fire, because it was baking day, and made up a blazing fire; and just as the wolf was coming down, took off the cover and in fell the Wolf. So the little Pig put on the cover again in an instant, boiled him up and ate him for supper, and lived happy ever afterwards.

From A WONDER BOOK OF BEASTS

Mowgli's Brothers

RUDYARD KIPLING

IT was seven o'clock of a very warm evening in the Seeonee hills when Father Wolf woke up from his day's rest, scratched himself, yawned, and spread out his paws one after the other to get rid of the sleepy feeling in their tips. Mother Wolf lay with her big gray nose dropped across her four tumbling, squealing cubs, and the moon shone into the mouth of the cave where they all lived. "Augrh!" said Father Wolf, "it is time to hunt again"; and he was going to spring downhill when a little shadow with a bushy tail crossed the threshold and whined: "Good luck go with you, O Chief of the Wolves; and good luck and strong white teeth go with the noble children, that they may never forget the hungry in this world."

It was the Jackal—Tabaqui, the Dish-licker—and the wolves of India despise Tabaqui because he runs about making mischief, and telling tales, and eating rags and pieces of leather from the village rubbish heaps. But they are afraid of him too, because Tabaqui, more than any one else in the jungle, is apt to go mad, and then he forgets that he was ever afraid of anyone, and runs through the forest biting everything in his way. Even the tiger runs and hides when little Tabaqui goes mad, for madness is the most disgraceful thing that can overtake a wild creature. We call it hydrophobia but they call it *dewance*—the madness—and run.

"Enter, then, and look," said Father Wolf, stiffly, "but there is no food here."

"For a wolf, no," said Tabaqui; "but for so mean a person as myself a dry bone is a good feast. Who are we, the Gidur-log (the jackal-people) to pick and choose?" He scuttled to the back of the cave where he found the bone of a buck with some meat on it, and sat cracking the end merrily.

"All thanks for this good meal," he said, licking his lips. "How beautiful are the noble children! How large are their eyes! And so young too! Indeed, indeed, I might have remembered that the children of Kings are men from the beginning."

Now, Tabaqui knew as well as anyone else that there is nothing so unlucky as to compliment children to their faces; and it pleased him to see Mother and Father Wolf look uncomfortable.

Tabaqui sat still, rejoicing in the mischief that he had made: then he said spitefully:

"Shere Khan, the Big One, has shifted his hunting-grounds. He will hunt among these hills for the next moon, so he has told me."

Shere Khan was the tiger who lived near the Waingunga River, twenty miles away.

"He has no right!" Father Wolf began angrily—"By the law of the Jungle he has no right to change his quarters without due warning. He will frighten every head of game within ten miles, and I—I have to kill for two, these days."

"His mother did not call him Lungri (the Lame One) for nothing," said Mother Wolf quietly. "He has been lame in one foot from his birth. That is why he has only killed cattle. Now the villagers of the Waingunga are angry with him, and he has come here to make *our* villagers angry.

They will scour the jungle for him when he is far away, and we and our children must run when the grass is set alight. Indeed we are grateful to Shere Khan!"

"Shall I tell him of your gratitude?" said Tabaqui.

"Out!" snapped Father Wolf. "Out and hunt with thy master. Thou hast done enough harm for one night."

"I go," said Tabaqui quietly. "Ye can hear Shere Khan below in the thickets. I might have saved myself the message."

Father Wolf listened, and below in the valley that ran down to a little river, he heard the dry, angry, snarly, sing-song whine of a tiger who has caught nothing and does not care if all the jungle knows it.

"The fool!" said Father Wolf. "To begin a night's work with that noise! Does he think that our buck are like his fat Waingunga bullocks?"

"Hsh! It is neither bullock nor buck he hunts to-night," said Mother Wolf. " It is Man." The whine had changed to a sort of humming purr that seemed to come from every quarter of the compass. It was the noise that bewilders woodcutters and gipsies sleeping in the open, and makes them run sometimes into the very mouth of the tiger.

"Man!" said Father Wolf, showing all his white teeth. "Faugh! Are there not enough beetles and frogs in the tanks, that he must eat Man, and on our ground too!"

The Law of the Jungle, which never orders anything without a reason, forbids every beast to eat Man except when he is killing to show his children how to kill, and then he must hunt outside the hunting grounds of his pack or tribe. The real reason for this is that man-killing means, sooner or later, the arrival of white men on elephants, with guns, and hundreds of brown men with gongs and rockets and torches. Then everybody in the jungle suffers.

The reason the beasts give among themselves is that Man is the weakest and most defenceless of all living things, and it is unsportsmanlike to touch him. They say too—and it is true—that man-eaters become mangy, and lose their teeth.

The purr grew louder, and ended in the full-throated "Aaarh!" of the tiger's charge.

Then there was a howl—an untigerish howl—from Shere Khan. "He has missed," said Mother Wolf. "What is it?"

Father Wolf ran out a few paces and heard Shere Khan muttering and mumbling savagely, as he tumbled about in the scrub.

"The fool has had no more sense than to jump at a woodcutter's camp-fire, and has burned his feet," said Father Wolf, with a grunt. "Tabaqui is with him."

"Something is coming up hill," said Mother Wolf, twitching one ear. "Get ready."

The bushes rustled a little in the thicket, and Father Wolf dropped with his haunches under him, ready for his leap. Then, if you had been watching, you would have seen the most wonderful thing in the world—the wolf checked in mid-spring. He made his bound before he saw what he was jumping at, and then he tried to stop himself. The result was that he shot up straight into the air for four or five feet, landing almost where he left ground.

"Man!" he snapped. "A man's cub. Look!"

Directly in front of him, holding on by a low branch, stood a naked brown baby who could just walk—as soft and as dimpled a little atom as ever came to a wolf's cave at night. He looked up into Father Wolf's face, and laughed.

"Is that a man's cub?" said Mother Wolf. "I have never seen one. Bring it here."

A wolf accustomed to moving its own cubs can, if necessary, mouth an egg without breaking it, and though Father Wolf's jaws closed right on the child's back not a tooth even scratched the skin, as he laid it down among the cubs.

"How little! How naked, and—how bold!" said Mother Wolf softly. The baby was pushing his way between the cubs to get close to the warm hide. "Ahai! He is taking his meal with the others. And so this is man's cub. Now, was there ever a wolf that could boast of a man's cub among her children?"

"I have heard now and again of such a thing," said Father Wolf, "but never in our Pack or in my time. He is altogether without hair, and I could kill him with a touch of my foot. But see, he looks up and is not afraid."

The moonlight was blocked out of the mouth of the cave, for Shere Khan's great square head and shoulders were thrust into the entrance. Tabaqui, behind him, was squeaking: "My Lord, my Lord, it went in here!"

"Shere Khan does us great honour," said Father Wolf but his eyes were very angry. "What does Shere Khan need?"

"My quarry. A man's cub went this way," said Shere Khan. "Its parents have run off. Give it to me."

Shere Khan had jumped at a woodcutter's camp-fire, as Father Wolf had said, and was furious from the pain of his burned feet. But Father Wolf knew that the mouth of the cave was too narrow for a tiger to come in by. Even where he was, Shere Khan's shoulders and forepaws were cramped for want of room, as a man's would be if he tried to fight in a barrel.

"The Wolves are a free people," said Father Wolf. "They take orders from the Head of the Pack, and not

from any striped cattle-killer. The man's cub is ours—to kill if we choose."

"Ye choose and ye do not choose! What talk is this of choosing? By the bull that I killed, am I to stand nosing into your dog's den for my fair dues? It is I, Shere Khan, who speak!"

The tiger's roar filled the cave with thunder. Mother Wolf shook herself clear of the cubs and sprang forward, her eyes like two green moons in the darkness, facing the blazing eyes of Shere Khan.

"And it is I, Raksha (The Demon) who answer. The

man's cub is mine, Lungri—mine to me! He shall not be killed. He shall live to run with the pack and to hunt with the Pack; and in the end, look you, hunter of little naked cubs—frog-eater—fish-killer—he shall hunt *thee!* Now get hence, or by the Sambhur that I killed (I eat no starved cattle), back thou goest to thy mother, burned beast of the jungle, lamer than ever thou camest into the world! Go!"

Father Wolf looked on amazed. He had almost forgotten the days when he won Mother Wolf in fair fight from five other wolves, when she ran in the Pack and was not called The Demon for compliment's sake. Shere Khan might have faced Father Wolf, but he could not stand up against Mother Wolf, for he knew that where he was she had all the advantage of the ground, and would fight to the death. So he backed out of the cave-mouth growling, and when he was clear he shouted:

"Each dog barks in his own yard! We will see what the Pack will say to this fostering of man-cubs. The cub is mine, and to my teeth he will come in the end, O bush-tailed thieves!"

Mother Wolf threw herself now panting among the cubs, and Father Wolf said to her gravely:

"Shere Khan speaks this much truth. The cub must be shown to the Pack. Wilt thou still keep him, Mother?"

"Keep him!" she gasped. "He came naked by night, alone and very hungry; yet he was not afraid! Look, he has pushed one of my babes to one side already. And that lame butcher would have killed him and would have run off to the Waingunga while the villagers here hunted through all our lairs in revenge! Keep him? Assuredly I will keep him. Lie still, little frog. O thou Mowgli—for Mowgli the frog I will call thee—the time will come when thou wilt hunt Shere Khan as he has hunted thee."

"But what will our Pack say?" said Father Wolf.

The Law of the Jungle lays down very clearly that any wolf may, when he marries, withdraw from the Pack he belongs to; but as soon as his cubs are old enough to stand on their feet he must bring them to the Pack Council, which is generally held once a month at full moon, in order that the other wolves may identify them. After that inspection the cubs are free to run where they please, and until they have killed their first buck no excuse is accepted if a grown wolf of the Pack kills one of them. The punishment is death where the murderer can be found, and if you think for a minute you will see that this must be so.

Father Wolf waited until his cubs could run a little, and then on the night of the Pack Meeting took them and Mowgli and Mother Wolf to the Council Rock—a hilltop covered with stones and boulders where a hundred wolves could hide. Akela, the great gray Lone Wolf, who led all the Pack by strength and cunning, lay out at full length on his rock, and below him sat forty or more wolves of every size and colour, from badger-coloured veterans who could handle a buck alone, to young, black three-year-olds who thought they could. The Lone Wolf had led them for a year now. He had fallen twice into a wolf-trap in his youth and once he had been beaten and left for dead; so he knew the manners and customs of men. There was very little talking at the Rock. The cubs tumbled over each other in the centre of the circle where their mothers and fathers sat, and now and again a senior wolf would go quietly up to a cub, look at him carefully, and return to his place on noiseless feet. Sometimes a mother would push her cub far out into the moonlight, to be sure that he had not been overlooked. Akela from his rock would cry: "Ye know the Law—ye know the Law. Look well, O Wolves!" and the anxious mothers would take up the call: "Look—look well, O Wolves!"

At last—and Mother Wolf's neck-bristles lifted as the time came—Father Wolf pushed "Mowgli the Frog" as they called him, into the centre, where he sat laughing and playing with some pebbles that glistened in the moonlight.

Akela never raised his head from his paws, but went on with the monotonous cry: "Look well!" A muffled roar came up from behind the rocks—the voice of Shere Khan crying: "The cub is mine. Give him to me. What have the Free People to do with a man's cub?" Akela never even twitched his ears; all he said was: "Look well, O Wolves! What have the Free People to do with the orders of any save the Free People? Look well!"

There was a chorus of deep growls, and a young wolf in his fourth year flung back Shere Khan's question to Akela: "What have the Free People to do with a man's cub?" Now the law of the jungle lays down that if there is any dispute as to the right of a cub to be accepted by the Pack, he must be spoken for by at least two members of the Pack who are not his father and mother.

"Who speaks for this cub?" said Akela. "Among the Free People who speaks?" There was no answer, and Mother Wolf got ready for what she knew would be her last fight, if things came to fighting.

Then the only other creature that is allowed at the Pack Council—Baloo, the sleepy brown bear who teaches the wolf cubs the Law of the Jungle: old Baloo, who can come and go where he pleases because he eats only nuts and roots and honey—rose up on his hind quarters and grunted.

"The man's cub—the man's cub?" he said. "I speak for the man's cub. There is no harm in a man's cub. I have no gift of words, but I speak the truth. Let him run with the

Pack, and be entered with the others. I myself will teach him."

"We need yet another," said Akela. "Baloo has spoken, and he is our teacher for the young cubs. Who speaks besides Baloo?"

A black shadow dropped down into the circle. It was Bagheera the black Panther, inky black all over, but with the panther markings showing up in certain lights like the pattern of watered silk. Everbody knew Bagheera and nobody cared to cross his path; for he was as cunning as Tabaqui, as bold as the wild buffalo, and as reckless as the wounded elephant. But he had a voice as soft as wild honey dripping from a tree, with a skin softer than down.

"O Akela, and ye the Free People," he purred, "I have no right in your assembly; but the Law of the Jungle says that if there is a doubt which is not a killing matter in regard to a new cub, the life of that cub may be bought at a price. And the Law does not say who may or may not pay that price. Am I right?"

"Good! Good!" said the young wolves, who are always hungry. "Listen to Bagheera. The cub can be bought for a price. It is the Law."

"Knowing that I have no right to speak here, I ask your leave."

"Speak, then," cried twenty voices.

"To kill a naked cub is a shame. Besides, he may be better sport for you when he is grown. Baloo has spoken in his behalf. Now to Baloo's words I will add one bull, and a fat one, newly killed, not half a mile from here, if ye will accept the man's cub according to the Law. Is it difficult?"

There was a clamour of scores of voices, saying: "What matter? He will die in the winter rains. He will scorch in the sun. What harm can a naked frog do us? Let him run with the Pack. Where is the bull, Bagheera? Let him be accepted." And then came Akela's deep bay, crying "Look well—look well, O Wolves!"

Mowgli was still deeply interested in the pebbles, and he did not notice when the wolves came and looked at him one by one. At last they all went down the hill for the dead bull, and only Akela, Bagheera, Baloo and Mowgli's own wolves were left. Shere Khan roared still in the night, for he was very angry that Mowgli had not been handed over to him.

"Ay, roar well," said Bagheera, under his whiskers, "for the time comes when this naked thing will make thee roar to another tune, or I know nothing of man."

"It was well done," said Akela. "Men and their cubs are very wise. He may be a help in time."

"Truly, a help in time of need; for none can hope to lead the Pack forever," said Bagheera.

Akela said nothing. He was thinking of the time that comes to every leader of every pack when his strength goes from him and he gets feebler and feebler, till at last he is killed by the wolves and a new leader comes up—to be killed in his turn.

"Take him away," he said to the Father Wolf, "and train him as befits one of the Free People."

And that is how Mowgli was entered into the Seeonee wolf-pack at the price of a bull and on Baloo's good word.

From THE JUNGLE BOOK

The Dog and the Wolf

AESOP

A LEAN, hungry, half-starved Wolf happened, one moonlight night, to meet with a jolly, plump, well-fed Dog. After the fiirst compliments were passed the Wolf said :

"You look extremely well; I protest, I think I never saw a more graceful, comely person. How comes it, I beseech you, that you should live so much better than I? I may say without vanity that I venture fifty times more than you do and yet I am almost ready to perish with hunger."

The Dog answered very bluntly:

"Why, you may live as well, if you will do the same as I do."

"Indeed! What is that?" said he.

"Why," said the Dog, "only to guard the house anights and keep it from thieves."

"With all my heart," replied the Wolf, "for at present I have but a sorry time of it, and to change my hard lodging in the woods where I endure rain, frost and snow, for a warm roof over my head and a belly-full of good victuals, will be no bad bargain."

"True," said the Dog, "therefore you have nothing more to do but to follow me."

Now as they were jogging on together the Wolf spied a crease in the Dog's neck and having a strange curiosity could not forbear asking what it meant.

"Pugh! nothing," said the Dog.

"Nay, but pray," said the Wolf.

"Why," said the Dog, "if you must know, I am tied up in the daytime because I am a little fierce and may bite people, and am only let loose at nights. But this is done with design to make me sleep during the day more than anything else, and as soon as the twilight appears, out I am turned and may go where I please. Then my master brings me plates of bones from the table with his own hands; and whatever scraps are left by any of the family, all fall to my share, for you must know I am a favourite with everybody. So you see how you are to live. Come, come along. What is the matter with you?"

"No," replied the Wolf, "I beg your pardon, keep your happiness to yourself. Liberty is the word with me, and I would not be a king upon the terms you mention."

Application: The lowest condition of life with freedom attending it, is better than the most exalted station under restraints.

AESOP: translation either Croxhall (1722) or James (1848)

Rollicum Bitem the Fox

JOHN MASEFIELD

John Masefield loved the English countryside as much as he loved ships. In The Midnight Folk *he tells how Kay finds out that his governess is a witch, up to no good as witches tend to be, and with the help of the house cat and the fox and some others he manages to outwit her and her gang, and restore the stolen treasure of the Cathedral of Santa Barbara. Nibbins is the good house cat—there is a wicked one too, named Blackmalkin—and in this piece he takes Kay to visit Rollicum Bitem the fox, in his den. They fly there on magic broomsticks which they steal from the witches. Nibbins and Kay become great friends. There is a very good Rat in this story too, but he can't afford to be friends with anyone.*

"THIS is where my friend lives, if he's not on his rounds," Nibbins said.

He led the way towards the quarry end, where there was much tumbled stone worn into a track by feet. A warm, strong scent was blowing about the place, more like a taste than a smell. The ground was white with little bones. Something that looked like washing hung upon the gorse bushes; it was not washing, though; it was rabbit skins hung up to dry. Someone with a most unpleasant voice was doing something with the rabbit skins, and singing as he worked; he was either folding the dry ones or hanging more fresh.

His song was not a nice one.

"I crept out of covert and what did I see?
Ow-ow-ow-diddle-ow!
But seven fat bunnies, each waiting for me.
With a poacher's noosey, catch the fat goosey, Ho says
Rollicum Bitem.

" 'O pretty bunnies, let's come for a stroll.'
'O no, no, no; you're a fox.'
'A fox, pretty dears; can't you see I'm a mole?'
With a weaselly, stoaty, snap at his throaty, Ho says
Rollicum Bitem.

" 'Let's dance, one by one, arm in arm, as dear friends.'
'O certainly, sir, if you please.'
So seven fat bunnies had seven sweet ends . . . .
Hay for a hennerel, snug in my dennerel, Ho says
Rollicum Bitem."

The song stopped suddenly. Kay heard no sound of footsteps but suddenly two very bright green eyes were shining at him above some glittering teeth.

"It's all right, Bitem, old boy," Nibbins said. "It's only Nibs. This is my friend, Kay. Mr. Kay, Mr. Lightfoot, Mr. Rollicum Bitem Lightfoot."

"Oh, it's you, Nibs! Pleased to meet you, Mr. Kay. Come in, won't you? Sorry I didn't recognise you at once. This way." He led the way to what looked like the mouth of a cave in the quarry face. "It will be dark for you," he said to Kay. "You'll find some glow-worms on the shelf there, if you want a light."

Kay took a glow-worm from the shelf; by the light of this he was able to see where he was going. The two others went down the passage in front of him. It was a rough, dark, narrow passage, with many twists in it. Everywhere there was this strong, rich scent, so like a taste. There were many rabbit skins about, as well as feathers.

"Mr. Bitem deals in game," Nibbins said. "I have to consult him about some rabbiting."

Mr. Bitem led them into his study, which was also his bedroom and larder. "Bachelor's quarters," he said. "A bit rough-and-ready but then I'm only here in the winter, really. Would you care to pick a wing or anything? No? I've some nice fowl, cold; and there's a bit of duck under the floor there. No? Well, what do you want with me, Nibs?"

"About our rabbiting to-morrow night, Bitem. Of course, you can speak freely before Mr. Kay. . . . I rather think my cousin Blackmalkin has betrayed us to the keeper. I happened to see him come from the keeper's cottage; I was up in a tree among some ivy. He came out, licking his lips, for he'd been having milk. He didn't see me; he passed just underneath me, but I heard him chuckle to himself and say: 'Keeper will get the lot of them,' You see, Kay, my two cousins, Blackmalkin and Greymalkin, and myself, have been in this midnight business together for quite a long time. Well, lately we've been helping Bitem in the game industry, on quiet nights, after new moon, and so on; and we had planned a big hunt for to-morrow, out Coneycop Spinney way: a really big hunt; ourselves Bitem and some of his relatives . . . . now Blackmalkin has not been dependable for a long time. This magic business is very bad for a fellow, and he is in it deeply, with a very bad set, all the Pouncer Seven. You mark my words, he has been put up by the Seven to betray us to the keeper.

"When he had gone, I crept down from my tree, got into Keeper's cottage, and upstairs under the bed. Presently

Keeper came in with those nasty dogs of his, and put his gun on the rack. 'I've got some news for you, my dear,' his wife said. 'Here's Blackmalkin just come in to say that there's a big rabbit drive arranged for Friday night in the Spinney; that Bitem lot and his cousins are in it."

" 'I'll rabbit 'em,' Keeper said. You know his coarse, red way. 'I'll rabbit 'em.'

" 'Yes, my dear,' his wife said, 'Blackmalkin said you'd get the lot of them. Of course after what he'd told me, I gave him some milk and that bit of sardine that there was.'

" 'Quite right,' Keeper said. 'If I get the lot of them, he shall have more than milk and sardine. He shall have Long Tail's Wing.'

" 'O hush, my dear,' his wife said; 'somebody might hear you.'

" 'Tut! nobody can hear me,' Keeper said, blowing out

his big lips. 'But I'll rabbit 'em. Let 'em come on Friday, I'll ask no better.' Then he went out and began oiling his gun; I could hear him singing:

"'I'll get him oiled for Friday,
So it shall be their die-day,
And Satter-day
Shall be Batter-day,
And Sunday hot rabbit-pie day.'

"I had to wait in the room for hours, because his nasty dogs were in the room below; but at last I could stand it no longer; I made a dart for the chimney, and was over the roof and into the pines before the dogs were upstairs. I heard Keeper ask, 'What's the matter with the dogs?' and his wife said 'It sounded like a young jackdaw got down into the chimney again.' 'I'll jackdaw them jackdaws one

of these days,' he said, 'if they keep on jackdawing me.' 'That's that,' she said. So that was that, and here I am."

"Ha," Bitem said, "so that's that for to-morrow's hunt. Now what can we do for Blackmalkin? Of all the traitors I ever did hear of! But we'll pretend we're going, up to the last. Keeper and the beaters will all be at Coneycop, waiting for us. And we'll send Blackmalkin there. But we, ourselves, will go off and draw out Brady Ride way: there's pretty toothing in the rabbit there, especially in the South Warren. And Keeper and beaters will wait all night for us at Coneycop; and when they learn that we've been at Brady, they'll pretty well have it out of Blackmalkin for misleading them. They'll toss him in a gamebag, and serve him right."

"I say, you have got a brain, Bitem," Nibbins said. "I knew you'd have a plan at once. That's the advantage of working with you; never at a loss: I never saw such a fellow."

"A fellow had need to be never at a loss," Bitem said. "The huntsmen are bad enough, in their red coats, but at least you do expect a keeper to stand your friend."

"If you wouldn't mind just moving to the door, Kay," Nibbins said, "Bitem and I could map out our hunt a bit, using the floor as a map."

Kay moved to the door. He watched them as they put rabbit-skins and feathers on the ground to mark places in the wood. He listened to them for a few minutes.

"This hen's head is the big yew. That rabbit-skin is the boggy patch; you know the place. Then here is where we got the partridge chicks. I'll put this pheasant's tail to mark the end of the South Warren. Hob Ferret'll join in there, and Jill will come if we want her. Then you will steal up here . . . . and I will steal up there . . . . Yes, and then Greymalkin is awfully good at a drop-pounce. Then we'll all go over and down to North Warren . . . ."

Kay grew weary of all this talk, because he had never been to Brady Ride Wood; he strolled quietly along the passage towards its mouth in the quarry face. He put back the glow worm on the ledge, and peeped out of the entrance.

He drew back at once, because there, in the quarry, not far from the cave, was a man at work among the stones. He was kneeling in a patch of shadow, but his face came up into the moonlight from time to time.

Kay saw from his velveteen coat that it was the Keeper.

"What on earth is he doing?" Kay wondered.

Presently the Keeper stood up to stretch his back. He was wearing gloves. He drew from a sack a big iron snap-trap, which he opened and set among the stones in the middle of the path leading to Bitem's earth. When it was set, he very cleverly and cautiously strewed it over with moss, dead grass, leaves and earth.

"That will catch your light feet, Mr. Lightfoot," he said; "and then, with my good gun, I'll put an end to your snibbing of my rabbits. Many a young hunter will give a pound for that mask of yourn, and your brush shall be a cobweb cleaner before you're a week older. I'll get up my tree, my master, and watch till you walk click into it. You'll be coming home within an hour. I know your ways."

Kay saw him move into the wood above the quarry, where he began to climb a tree. As soon as he was climbing, Kay hurried back to tell the others what he had seen.

"A trap?" Bitem said; "and Keeper watching from a tree? I am very much obliged to you, Mr. Kay. I must be gone from here by the secret door. I'll move off to my place Wicked Hill way."

"There's something on at Wicked Hill, the owls said," Nibbins said. "Do you think it would be safe?"

"A lot safer than this," Bitem said.

"Yes, for you," Nibbins said. "But I meant for us."

"They don't harm anyone that keeps outside the magic circle."

"I'd love to go, just to look on," Nibbins said. "It's probably a big magic night, Kay, when they have a bon-fire; and oh, I do love to see them at magic. It's terrifying, but I can't resist it."

"Well, come along," Bitem said.

"We can steal round to our horses and give you a lift, Bitem."

The fox led the way out of his study into the narrow passage where Kay had to crawl on hands and knees. This led into a biggish room from which several passages branched; water was dripping in one of them.

"Very convenient in here," Bitem said. "Lots of ways out and plenty of water; but this is the way we'll take to-night."

From THE MIDNIGHT FOLK

Singh Rajah and the Cunning Little Jackals

MARY FRERE

ONCE upon a time, in a great jungle, there lived a great Lion. He was Rajah of all the country around, and every day he used to leave his den in the deepest shadow of the rocks, and roar with a loud, angry voice. And when he had roared, the other animals in the jungle, who were all his subjects, got very much frightened and ran here and there; and Singh Rajah, the Lion King, would pounce upon them and kill them, and gobble them up for his dinner.

This went on for a long, long time, until at last there were no living creatures left in the jungle but two little Jackals—a Rajah Jackal, and a Ranee Jackal, husband and wife.

A very hard time of it the poor little Jackals had, running this way and that to escape the terrible Singh Rajah; and every day the little Ranee Jackal would say to her husband:

"I am afraid he will catch us to-day. Do you hear how he is roaring? Oh dear! oh dear!"

And he would answer her:

"Never fear, I will take care of you. Let us run a mile or two. Come, come—quick, quick, quick!"

And they would both run away as fast as they could.

After some time spent this way, they found, however, one fine day, that the Lion was so close upon them that they could not escape. Then the little Ranee Jackal said:

"Husband, husband, I feel very frightened! The Singh Rajah is so angry, he will certainly kill us at once. What can we do?"

But he answered:

"Cheer up; we can save ourselves yet. Come, and I'll show you how we can manage it."

So what did those cunning little Jackals do, but they went to the great Lion's den; and when he saw them coming, he began to roar and shake his mane, and he said:

"You little wretches, come and be eaten at once! I have had no dinner for three whole days, and all that time I have been running over hill and dale to find you. Ro-a-r! Ro-a-r! Come and be eaten, I say!" and he lashed his tail and gnashed his teeth; and looked very terrible indeed.

Then the Jackal Rajah, creeping quite close up to him said:

"O great Singh Rajah, we all know you are our master, and we would have come at your bidding long ago; but indeed, sir, there is a much bigger lion even than you in this jungle, and he tried to catch hold of us and eat us up, and frightened us so much that we were obliged to run away."

"What do you mean?" growled Singh Rajah. "There is no king in this jungle but me!"

"Ah, Sire," answered the Jackal, "in truth, one would think so, for you are very dreadful. Your very voice is death. But it is as we say, for we, with our own eyes, have seen one with whom you could not compete; whose equal you can no more be than we are yours; whose face is as the flaming fire, his step as thunder, and his power supreme."

"It is impossible!" interrupted the old Lion. "But show

me this Rajah of whom you speak so much, that I may destroy him instantly."

Then the little Jackals ran on before him until they reached a great well, and pointing down to his own reflection in the water, they said:

"See, Sire, there lives the terrible king of whom we spoke."

When Singh Rajah looked down into the well, he became very angry, for he thought he saw another Lion there. He roared and shook his great mane, and the shadow Lion shook his, and looked terribly defiant. At last, beside himself with rage at the insolence of his opponent, Singh Rajah sprang down to kill him at once, but no other Lion was there—only the treacherous reflection; and the sides of the well were so steep that he could not get out again to punish the two Jackals, who peeped over the top. After struggling for some time in the deep water, he sank to rise no more. And the little Jackals threw stones down upon him from above, and danced round and round the well singing:

"Ao! Ao! Ao! Ao! The King of the Forest is dead! We have killed the great Lion who would have killed us! Ao! Ao! Ao! Ao! Ring-a-ting—ding-a-ting! Ring-a-ting—ding-a-ting! Ao! Ao! Ao!"

From THE WONDER BOOK OF BEASTS

The Fox, the Wolf and the Mule

This story is taken from a collection made in Florence at the end of the fourteenth century. Most of the other stories are about Kings and Popes and Saints and Soldiers, and some are ancient stories about gods and goddesses, retold in the Florentine dialect of the time.

THE Fox was taking a walk in a wood one day when he saw a Mule, and never in his life had he seen the like before. He was greatly frightened, and his first thought was to fly for his life. As he galloped along, who should he see but the Wolf, and told him that he had seen a new beast whose name he did not know. The Wolf said at once:

"Let's go. I'm all for seeing this beast."

They found the Mule, and the Wolf was astonished: he had never seen such a beast either.

The Wolf swaggered up and asked the Mule his name. The Mule answered:

"I'm afraid I just can't remember it at this moment. But if you are able to read, you'll find it written on one of my hind hooves."

"That's too bad," said the Fox. "If I knew how to read, I'd find out your name in two shakes."

"Let me have a look," said the Wolf. "I'm well able to read."

The Mule lifted up his hoof so that the underside showed, and the nails looked exactly like letters.

"I can't see it properly," said the Wolf.

"Come a little nearer," said the Mule. "The letters are very small."

Trustingly the Wolf came closer, until he was right underneath the Mule's hoof, gazing up at it. The Mule made a swipe with his hoof and kicked the Wolf on the head, killing him stone dead.

The Fox cleared off, saying to himself:

"Not everyone who can read is wise."

Translated from the Italian by EILÍS DILLON

The Twa Corbies

ANON

As I was walking all alane
I heard twa corbies making a mane,
The tane unto the t'other say,
"Where sall we gang and dine to-day?"

"In behind yon auld fail dyke
I wot there lies a new-slain Knight;
And naebody kens that he lies there
But his hawk, his hound and his lady fair.

"His hound is to the hunting gane,
His hawk to fetch the wild-fowl hame,
His lady's ta'en another mate,
So we may mak' our dinner sweet.

"Ye'll sit on his white hause-bane,
And I'll pick out his bonny blue een:
Wi' ae lock o' his gowden hair
We'll theek our nest when it grows bare.

"Mony a one for him makes mane,
But none sall ken where he is gane;
O'er his white banes, when they are bare,
The wind sall blaw for evermair."

Proud Maisie

SIR WALTER SCOTT

Proud Maisie is in the wood,
Walking so early;
Sweet robin sits on the bush
Singing so rarely.

"Tell me, thou bonny bird,
When shall I marry me?"
—"When six braw gentlemen
Kirkward shall carry ye."

"Who makes the bridal bed,
Birdie, say truly?"
—"The gray-headed sexton
That delves the grave duly.

"The glow-worm o'er grave and stone
Shall light thee steady;
The owl from the steeple sing
Welcome, proud lady."

The Pets

ROBERT FARREN

Colm had a cat
  and a wren,
  and a fly.

The cat was a pet,
  and the wren,
  and the fly.

And it happened that the wren
  ate the fly;
  and it happened that the cat
  ate the wren.

Then the cat died.

So Colm lacked a cat
  and a wren,
  and a fly.

But Saint Colm loved the cat,
  and the wren,
  and the fly,

so he prayed to get them back,
  cat and wren,
  and he prayed to get them back,
  wren and fly.

And the cat became alive
  and delivered up the wren;
  and the wren became alive
  and delivered up the fly;
  and they all lived with Colm
  till the day came to die.

First the cat died.
  Then the wren died.
  Then the fly.

How Some Wild Animals Became Tame Ones

ANDREW LANG

ONCE upon a time there lived a miller who was so rich that, when he was going to be married, he asked to the feast not only his own friends but also the wild animals who dwelt in the hills and woods round about. The chief of the bears, the wolves, the foxes, the horses, the cows, the goats, the sheep and the reindeer, all received invitations; and as they were not accustomed to weddings they were greatly pleased and flattered, and sent back messages in the politest language that they would certainly be there.

The first to start on the morning of the wedding-day was the bear, who always liked to be punctual; and besides, he had a long way to go, and his hair, being so thick and rough, needed a good brushing before it was fit to be seen at a party. However, he took care to awaken very early, and set off down the road with a light heart. Before he had walked very far he met a boy who came whistling along, hitting at the tops of the flowers with a stick.

"Where are you going?" said he looking at the bear in surprise, for he was an old acquaintance, and not generally so smart.

"Oh, just to the miller's marriage," answered the bear carelessly. "Of course, I would rather stay at home, but the

miller was so anxious that I should be there that I really could not refuse."

"Don't go, don't go!" cried the boy. "If you do you will never come back! You have got the most beautiful skin in the world—just the kind that everyone is wanting and they will be sure to kill you and strip you of it."

"I had not thought of that," said the bear, whose face

turned white, only nobody could see it. "If you are certain that they would be so wicked—but perhaps you are jealous because nobody has invited *you*?"

"Oh, nonsense!" replied the boy angrily, "do as you please. It is your skin and not mine. *I* don't care what becomes of it!" And he walked quickly on with his head in the air.

The bear waited until he was out of sight and then followed him slowly, for he felt in his heart that the boy's advice was good, though he was too proud to say so.

The boy soon grew tired of walking along the road and and turned off into the woods, where there were bushes he could jump and streams he could wade; but he had not gone far before he met the wolf.

"Where are you going?" asked he, for it was not the first time he had seen him.

"Oh, just to the miller's marriage," answered the wolf, as the bear had done before him. "It is rather tiresome, of course—weddings are always so stupid; but still one must be good-natured!"

"Don't go!" said the boy again. "Your skin is so thick and warm, and winter is not far off now. They will kill you and strip it from you."

The wolf's jaw dropped in astonishment and terror.

"Do you *really* think that would happen?" he gasped.

"Yes, to be sure I do," answered the boy. "But it is your affair, not mine. So good morning," and on he went.

The wolf stood still for a few minutes, for he was trembling all over, and then crept quietly back to his cave.

Next the boy met the fox, whose lovely coat of silvery grey was shining in the sun.

"You look very fine," said the boy, stopping to admire him. "Are you going to the miller's wedding too?"

"Yes," answered the fox. "It is a long journey to take for such a thing as that, but you know what the miller's friends are like—so dull and heavy! It is only kind to go and amuse them a little."

"You poor fellow," said the boy pityingly. "Take my advice and stay at home. If you once enter the miller's gate, his dogs will tear you to pieces."

"Ah, well, such things have occurred," replied the fox gravely.

And without saying any more he trotted off the way he had come.

His tail had scarcely disappeared, when a great noise of crashing branches was heard, and up bounded the horse, his black skin glistening like satin.

"Good morning," he called to the boy as he galloped past, "I can't wait to talk to you now. I have promised the miller to be present at his wedding feast, and they won't sit down till I come."

"Stop! Stop!" cried the boy after him, and there was something in his voice that made the horse pull up.

"What is the matter?" asked he.

"You don't know what you are doing," said the boy. "If once you go there, you will never gallop through these woods any more. You are stronger than many men, but they will catch you and put ropes around you, and you will have to work and serve them all the days of your life."

The horse threw back his head at these words and laughed scornfully.

"Yes, I am stronger than many men," answered he, "and all the ropes in the world would not hold me. Let them bind me as fast as they will, I can always break loose, and return to the forest and freedom."

And with this proud speech he gave a whisk of his long tail and galloped away faster than before.

But when he reached the miller's house everything happened as the boy had said. While he was looking at the guests and thinking how much handsomer and stronger he was than any of them, a rope was suddenly flung over his head, and he was thrown down and a bit thrust between his teeth. Then, in spite of his struggles, he was dragged to a stable, and shut up for several days without any food, till his spirit was broken and his coat had lost its gloss. After that he was harnessed to a plough, and had plenty of time to remember all he had lost through not listening to the counsel of the boy.

When the horse had turned a deaf ear to his words the boy wandered idly along, sometimes gathering wild strawberries from a bank, and sometimes plucking wild cherries from a tree, till he reached a clearing in the middle of the forest. Crossing this open space was a beautiful milk-white cow with a wreath of flowers around her neck.

"Good-morning," she said pleasantly as she came up to the place where the boy was standing.

"Good-morning," he returned. "Where are you going in such a hurry?"

"To the miller's wedding; I am rather late already, for the wreath took such a long time to make, so I can't stop."

"Don't go," said the boy earnestly. "When once they have tasted your milk they will never let you leave them, and you will have to serve them all the days of your life."

"Oh, nonsense! What do you know about it?" answered the cow, who always thought she was wiser than other people. "Why, I can run twice as fast as any of them! I should like to see anybody trying to keep me against my will."

And without even a polite bow, she went on her way, feeling very much offended.

But everything turned out just as the boy had said. The company had all heard of the fame of the cow's milk, and persuaded her to give them some, and then her doom was sealed. A crowd gathered round her, and held her horns so that she could not use them, and like the horse she was shut in the stable, and only let out in the mornings, when a long rope was tied round her head, and she was fastened to a stake in a grassy meadow.

And so it happened to the goat and the sheep.

Last of all came the reindeer, looking as he always did, as if some serious business was in hand.

"Where are you going?" asked the boy, who by this time was tired of wild cherries and was thinking of his dinner.

"I am invited to the wedding," answered the reindeer, "and the miller has begged me on no account to fail him."

"O fool!" cried the boy, "have you no sense at all? Don't you know that when you get there they will hold you fast, for neither beast nor bird is as strong nor as swift as you?"

"That is exactly why I am quite safe," replied the reindeer. "I am so strong that no one can bind me, and so swift that not even an arrow can catch me. So good-bye for the present. You will soon see me back."

But none of the animals that went to the miller's wedding ever came back. And because they were self-willed and conceited, and would not listen to good advice, they and their children have been the servants of men to this very day.

From THE BROWN FAIRY BOOK

Kpo the Leopard

RENÉ GUILLOT

This is one of René Guillot's best African animal stories. Kpo's mother dies and the young leopard is first adopted by a cheetah family and then captured by a young chieftain. He brings her to his house and treats her so well that she becomes deeply attached to him. She stays by him without moving until he recovers from injuries received at a lion hunt, but when he is well again, she feels the call of the jungle and sets off by night to find her way to the leopards' hunting grounds, bound to follow her instinct though she still loves the boy who brought her to safety.

"KPO!"

She purred when he said her name and it was a friendly sound which meant 'I am here'; and there she was, indeed, sitting beside her master, as attentive as ever, on a mat by the low bed where Amastan lay. She stayed by him constantly, always vigilant, never moving, and the look in her green, half-closed eyes rather frightened the young prince's friends when they came to ask news of him or stay with him and talk.

Even Taitok, the only one the leopard would sometimes allow to stroke her, had been frightened by that look of hers during those long weeks when Amastan's life was in the balance. All through those interminable days and nights of fever, when the boy lay trembling and unconscious, moaning feebly hour after hour, the two green lamps of Kpo's eyes had burned on like nightlights at the head of Amastan's bed.

The whole encampment had feared for the young prince's life. Taitok had stayed for hours by his master watching his face for some sign of movement, if only the flutter of an eyelid. Death was abroad then; death, creeping up stealthily, silent as a wolf, nearer and nearer. . . . Taitok saw Kpo, erect as a statue, turn her head slowly away from the poor, grey, wasted face and stare fixedly with wide open eyes at the big brown screen of hide which hung down over the entrance of the tent.

The dogs had stopped barking.

For a long, tense moment Kpo stood listening, trembling. Then she had turned back to her vigil, rested her eyes once more on Amastan and began to purr her friendly purr again.

"Kpo?" Yes, she was there. She was always there.

A little while ago they had brought a skin of fresh water and cloths to moisten and bandage his wounds, and Kpo had stood there patiently and watched as it was done, for had not Amastan tended her wounds in the same way when he took the spear out of her shoulder?

Amastan could take a little nourishment now and before going to sleep he drank a bowl of camel's milk which the faithful Taitok held to his lips. The bowl was just like the one Amastan used to bring for Kpo when she was recovering from her fever and her wound was healing.

In friendship everything comes round again; then the kindness done can be returned, and in one way or another one spends the hoarded gratitude. Joy or sorrow—all is shared in friendship. This was Kpo's way of returning all the love the boy had given her when she had been wounded and he had been her nurse.

The last two days Amastan had been able to get up. Yesterday he had walked a few steps around his tent. He had gone over and looked at his weapons and saddle set on the wooden chest, and at the black silk band which was also there, and the silver whistle.

Amastan lifted the whistle to his lips, and sounded Siho's hunting cry. As he stroked Kpo's great head he said to her: "We'll soon be hunting together again."

And now, to-day, he was going for his first walk outside. He left the tent, leaning on Taitok's arm. First he went to visit his father. The Emir was very proud of his son since the lion-hunt—indeed the whole tribe looked upon him as a hero, and there was general rejoicing now that he was getting well. For he had proved himself to be worthy of his father's noble line and there was now no doubt that he would be a great chief one day and could look forward to a magnificent reign over the proudest of the veiled tribes.

When Amastan visited the women's tent, they had prepared him a great welcome. All was singing and laughter. Tiliana took her little squeaky violin and accompanied Theia as she recited her most beautiful poem: the song of the wind and the Targui spear—that glorious spear that makes its own music with the strings of little metal buckles on the shaft which ring like tiny bells when you hold it high and race at full gallop into the wind on your *méhari*.

Kpo grew bored alone in the tent and went to look for Amastan, whom she found among the noble daughters of the *douar*.

The songs over, the girls had all gathered round Amastan and he had a smile for them all—he was very happy.

"Kpo will be jealous if you smile at us," teased Tiliana.

"Everyone knows that you love Kpo best," said the

dark Tina-Galuz, and her pretty teeth shone like pearls as she smiled.

But Amastan's tenderest smile was for Dassin. He spoke to her in a low voice and she laughed happily.

"Dassin," murmured Amastan.

"Amastan," murmured Dassin, and that was all the others heard.

Amastan was asleep. Kpo could hear his long, tranquil breathing. The young master's life was safe; no danger threatened him now. He was well on his way to recovery and Kpo had paid her debt.

It was not Kpo the dreamer who watched by him that night. Kpo had given up dreaming since her fight with the lion. Until that day—the whole time she had been with Amastan, whether in his tent or up behind him riding with the black band round her eyes, or racing off at the sound of the whistle over the dunes—Kpo had been neither cheetah nor leopard.

But now she had killed a lion and the ancient bush had restored to her the wild lust in her blood. Now Kpo was a leopard for good, a leopard of the southern woods, daughter of the night and of the lords of the Bau.

For a long time she sat licking her master's hand as it lay on the blankets and licking his forehead under its mop of black hair. He loved to feel her tongue on his face—indeed there was nothing she could do that would please him better. "Kpo, my beauty," he murmured in his sleep, and his voice was even gentler than when he whispered to Dassin.

Kpo's purring was broken by growls. She was both happy and angry, sad but resolute. In a corner of the tent were all the things which she had carried about in her mouth and played with: a round pebble, the silver whistle, her leash, Amastan's whip and a bracelet of blue shells and glass beads which had been Dassin's last present to him—a whole heap of Kpo's small toys. She looked them over and over, moving them with her paw as if counting them.

It was the same now, as she stood by the sleeping Amastan and looked at him for the last time: she seemed to be counting the happy days of friendship she had known with him—all as lovely and full of memories as the toys one puts aside.

All she took away with her in her mouth was the much-chewed silver whistle which still kept the smell of her master's hand.

Outside the usual restless noises stirred the night. The wind whistled over the tents, brushed up the fur of the dogs half buried in the sand, and blew chill among the penned camels, coughing and clearing their throats.

The tethered horses pulled on their head-ropes. The new courser which the Emir had given his son to replace Reïna was rubbing his nose against the nose of Taitok's white mare.

"Kpo's going away," said the mare.

The horses leered. "She'll come back," they said. Then they were silent as the leopard passed close to them on her way.

But this time there was no denying any longer the call of the wild that was pulsing through her veins since the fight in the desert when the king of the bush had bled to death beneath her claws. She was all leopard now and the forest was calling, calling. . . . There would be no more hunting for others. Not for her now the fair gazelles of the desert who played on the dunes like sand-fairies. This was their land, and Kpo was leaving it forever to go back to her own.

There were the gazelles now, just going by, some sauntering, some chasing each other, till they vanished in the mist like lovely pale shadows of the night.

Kpo was leaving her master, and she was leaving without regrets. . . .

Men could speak the gentlest of words with their mouths, and in their eyes was that magic water which makes their laughter shine. Many a time still, no doubt, Kpo would hear the beloved voice of Amastan ringing in her ears. But that night the wise bush silenced it. For the bush was recalling a daughter and it brought her other echoes of happiness to remind her of the happy days before her capture: the voice of Siho as she curled her tongue and uttered her hunting cry, the old father grumbling and spitting out chips of bone as he gnawed at his food, the little cheetah whimpering in his sleep and scratching her chest with his nails because he thought she was his mother.

Kpo was going away.

She crossed the first *shot* fields with long strides. She went round the dry well at the bottom of the sandy hollow. Two fenecs ferreting about round the stumps of sun-baked ethal-wood watched curiously as she went by. Here were the doom-palms, the spurges and mossy stones, and the plain of broken white shells.

And here was the first line of dunes.

Not once did Kpo look back. She went along with her nose to the ground, following the trail of the night which ran on and on, past the grey rocks of the cheetah tribe and away, still farther, to the southern lands, the forest and savanna where the Kri River flowed.

Night was leading her daughter back home.

But where was home? With the cheetahs?

No. With the leopards.

Kpo increased her pace.

At the foot of the second line of dunes she stopped. All that way she had had Amastan's little whistle in her mouth, which she had brought away as a souvenir of her life with men.

How she had loved that boy! One look from him and her heart swelled with joy and happiness. What friendship he had given her! And what boundless friendship she had given him in return!

Kpo let the little silver whistle fall on the sand and left it there. Of all that he had given her she had kept nothing—only the memory of his friendship. As she resumed her journey her heart was full; she would never forget the boy all the days of her life.

But it was a new life just beginning.

"Kpo. . . ."

She seemed to hear his voice. Perhaps he was calling her in his sleep back there in his tent. The rumble in her throat replied to him, as she stepped out even faster. . . .

"I shall always remember your friendship—the only one of your gifts I am taking with me."

From KPO THE LEOPARD

The Yak

HILAIRE BELLOC

As a friend to the children commend me the Yak.
   You will find it exactly the thing:
   It will carry and fetch, you can ride on its back,
   Or lead it around with a string.

The Tartar who dwells on the plains of Thibet
   (A desolate region of snow)
   Has for centuries made it a nursery pet,
   And surely the Tartar should know!

Then tell your papa where the Yak can be got,
   And if he is awfully rich
   He will buy you the creature—or else he will not,
   (I cannot be positive which.)

Jeoffry

CHRISTOPHER SMART

Christopher Smart, who wrote this poem about his cat, lived from 1722 to 1771. He was a journalist and a Fellow of Pembroke Hall in Oxford but he was always very poor. He was a great drinker, but very religious, and went mad in the end and had to be shut up in an asylum. His friends worried because they feared he would not get enough exercise there but Doctor Johnson said:

"No, Sir, he has partly as much exercise as he used to have. Indeed before his confinement, he used for exercise to walk to the alehouse; but he was carried back again." That sounds cruel but Doctor Johnson defended Smart on other occasions.

For I will consider my Cat Jeoffry,
For he is the servant of the Living God, duly and daily
  serving him.
For at the first glance of the glory of God in the East he
  worships in his way.
For is this done by wreathing his body seven times round
  with elegant quickness.
For then he leaps up to catch the musk, which is the bless-
  ing of God upon his prayer.
For he rolls upon prank to work it in.
For having done duty and received blessing he begins to
  consider himself.
For this he performs in ten degrees.
For first he looks upon his fore-paws to see if they are
  clean.

For secondly he kicks up behind to clear away there.
For thirdly he works it upon stretch with the forepaws extended.
For fourthly he sharpens his paws by wood.
For fifthly he washes himself.
For sixthly he rolls upon wash.
For seventhly he fleas himself, that he may not be interrupted upon the beat.
For eighthly he rubs himself against a post.
For ninthly he looks up for his instructions.
For tenthly he goes in quest of food.
For having considered God and himself he will consider his neighbour.
For if he meets another cat he will kiss her in kindness.
For when he takes his prey he plays with it to give it a chance.
For one mouse in seven escapes by his dallying.
For when his day's work is done his business more properly begins.
For he keeps the Lord's watch in the night against the adversary.
For he counteracts the powers of darkness by his electrical skin and glaring eyes.
For he counteracts the Devil, who is death, by brisking about the life.
For in his morning orisons he loves the sun and the sun loves him.
For he is of the tribe of the Tiger.
For the Cherub Cat is a term of the Angel Tiger.
For he has the subtlety and hissing of a serpent, which in goodness he suppresses.
For he will not do destruction, if he is well-fed, neither will he spit without provocation.

For he purrs in thankfulness, when God tells him he's
a good Cat.
For he is an instrument for the children to learn benevolence upon.
For every house is incompleat without him and a blessing
is lacking in the spirit.
For the Lord commanded Moses concerning the cats at
the departure of the Children of Israel from Egypt.
For every family had one cat at least in the bag.
For the English Cats are the best in Europe.
For he is the cleanest in the use of his fore-paws of any
quadrupede.
For the dexterity of his defence is an instance of the love
of God to him exceedingly.
For he is the quickest to his mark of any creature.
For he is tenacious of his point.
For he is a mixture of gravity and waggery.
For he knows that God is his Saviour.
For there is nothing sweeter than his peace when at rest.
For there is nothing brisker than his life when in
motion.
For he is of the Lord's poor and so indeed is he called by
benevolence perpetually—Poor Jeoffry! poor Jeoffry!
the rat has bit thy throat.
For I bless the name of the Lord Jesus that Jeoffry is
better.
For the divine spirit comes about his body to sustain it
in compleat cat.
For his tongue is exceedingly pure so that it has in purity
what it wants in musick.
For he is docile and can learn certain things.
For he can set up with gravity which is patience upon
approbation.

For he can fetch and carry, which is patience in employment.
For he can jump over a stick which is patience upon proof positive.
For he can spraggle upon waggle at the word of command.
For he can jump from an eminence into his master's bosom.
For he can catch the cork and toss it again.
For he is hated by the hypocrite and miser.
For the former is afraid of detection.
For the latter refuses the charge.
For he camels his back to bear the first notion of business.
For he is good to think on, if man would express himself neatly.
For he made a great figure in Egypt for his signal services.
For he killed the Icneumon-rat very pernicious by land.
For his ears are so acute that they sting again.
For from this proceeds the passing quickness of his attention.
For by stroaking of him I have found out electricity.
For I perceived God's light about him both wax and fire.
For the Electrical fire is the spiritual substance, which God sends from heaven to sustain the bodies both of man and beast.
For God has blessed him in the variety of his movements.
For, tho he cannot fly, he is an excellent clamberer.
For his motions upon the face of the earth are more than any other quadrupede.
For he can tread to all the measures upon the musick.
For he can swim for life.
For he can creep.

The Cunning Hare

ANDREW LANG

IN a very cold country, far across the seas, where ice and snow cover the ground for many months in the year, there lived a little hare who, as his father and mother were both dead, was brought up by his grandmother. As he was too young and she was too old to work, they were very poor, and often did not have enough to eat.

One day when the little fellow was hungrier than usual, he asked his grandmother if he might not go down to the river and catch a fish for their breakfast, as the thaw had come and the water was flowing freely again. She laughed at him for thinking that any fish would let itself be caught by a hare, especially such a young one; but as she had the rheumatism very badly, and could get no food herself, she let him go.

"If he does not catch a fish he may find something else," she said to herself.

So she told her grandson where to look for the net, and how he was to set it across the river; but just as he was starting, feeling himself quite a man, she called him back.

"After all, I don't know what is the use of your going, my boy. For even if you should catch a fish, I have no fire to cook it with."

"Let me catch my fish and I will soon make you a fire,"

he answered gaily, for he was young and knew nothing about the difficulties of fire-making.

It took him some time to haul the net through bushes and over fields but at length he reached a pool in the river which he had often heard was swarming with fish, and here he set his net as his grandmother had directed him.

He was so excited that he hardly slept all night, and at the very first streak of dawn he ran as fast as he could down to the river. His heart beat as quickly as if he had had dogs behind him, and he hardly dared to look lest he should be disappointed. Would there even be one fish? And at this thought the pangs of hunger made him feel quite sick with fear. But he need not have been afraid; in every mesh of the net there was a fine fat fish, and of course the net itself was so heavy that he could only lift one corner. He threw some of the fish back into the water and buried some more in a hole under a stone, where he would be sure to find them. Then he rolled up the net with the rest, put it on his back and carried it home. The weight of the load caused his back to ache, and he was thankful to drop it outside their hut, while he rushed in, full of joy to tell his grandmother.

"Be quick and clean them!" he said, "and I will go to those people's tents on the other side of the water."

The old woman stared at him in horror as she listened to his proposal. Other people had tried to steal fire before and few indeed had come back with their lives; but as, contrary to all her expectations, he had managed to catch such a number of fish, she thought that perhaps there was some magic about him which she did not know of, and did not try to hinder him.

When the fish were all taken out, he fetched the net which he had laid out to dry, folded it up very small and ran down to the river, hoping that he might find a place narrow enough for him to jump over; but he soon saw that it was too wide for even the best jumper in the world. For a few minutes he stood there, wondering what was to be done. Then there darted into his head some words of a spell which he had once heard a wizard use, while drinking from the river. He repeated them as well as he could remember, and waited to see what would happen. In five minutes such a grunting and a puffing was heard, and columns of water rose into the air, though he could not tell what had made them. Then round the bend of the stream came fifteen huge whales, which he ordered to place themselves head to tails like stepping stones, so that he could jump from one to the other till he landed on the opposite shore. Directly he got there he told the whales that he did not need them any more, and sat down on the sand to rest.

Unluckily some children who were playing about caught sight of him, and one of them, stealing softly up behind him, laid hold of his ears. The hare, who had been watching the whales as they sailed down the river, gave a violent start and struggled to get away. But the boy held on tight and ran back home as fast as he could go.

"Throw it in the pot," said the old woman as soon as he had told his story. "Put it in that basket and as soon as the water boils in the pot we will hang it over the fire!"

"Better kill it first," said the old man; and the hare listened, horribly frightened, but still looking secretly to see if there was no hole through which he could escape, if he had a chance of doing so. Yes, there was one, right in the top of the tent, so, shaking himself as if with fright, he let the end of his net unroll itself a little.

"I wish that a spark of fire would fall on my net,"

whispered he; and the next minute a great log fell forward into the midst of the tent, causing everyone to spring backwards. The sparks were scattered in every direction, and one fell on the net, making a little blaze. In an instant the hare had leaped through the hole, and was racing towards the river, with men, women and children after him. There was no time to call back the whales, so holding the net tight in his mouth, he wished himself across the river. Then he jumped high into the air and landed safe on the other side, and turning around to make sure that there was no chance of anyone pursuing him, trotted happily home to his grandmother.

"Didn't I tell you I would bring you fire?" said he, holding up his net, which was now burning briskly.

"But how did you cross the water?" inquired the old woman.

"Oh, I just jumped!" said he.

And his grandmother asked him no more questions, for she saw that he was wiser than she.

From THE BROWN FAIRY BOOK

Pivi and Kabo

ANDREW LANG

WHEN birds were men, and men were birds, Pivi and Kabo lived in an island far away, called New Caledonia. Pivi was a cheery little bird that chirps at sunset; Kabo was an ugly black fowl that croaks in the darkness. One day Pivi and Kabo thought that they would make slings, and practise slinging, as the people of that island still do. So they went to a banyan tree, and stripped the bark to make strings for their slings, and next they repaired to the river bank to find stones. Kabo stood on the bank of the river, and Pivi went into the water. The game was for Kabo to sling at Pivi, and for Pivi to dodge the stones if he could. For some time he dodged them cleverly but at last a stone from Kabo's sling hit poor Pivi on the leg and it broke. Down went Pivi into the stream, and floated along it, till he floated into a big hollow bamboo, which a woman used for washing her sweet potatoes.

"What is that in my bamboo?" said the woman. And she blew in at one end, and blew little Pivi out at the other like a pea from a pea-shooter.

"Oh!" cried the woman, "what a state you are in! What have you been doing?"

"It was Kabo who broke my leg at the slinging game," said Pivi.

"Well, I am sorry for you," said the woman; "will you come with me and do what I tell you?"

"I will!" said Pivi, for the woman was very kind and pretty.

She took Pivi into a shed where she kept her fruit, laid him on a bed of mats and made him as comfortable as she could, and attended to his broken leg without cutting off the flesh round the bone, as these people usually do.

"You will be still, Pivi, won't you?" she said. "If you hear a little noise you will pretend to be dead. It is the Black Ant who will come and creep from your feet up to your head. Say nothing, and keep quiet, won't you, Pivi?"

"Certainly, kind lady," said Pivi, "I will lie as still as can be."

"Next will come the big Red Ant—you know him?"

"Yes, I know him, with his feet like a grasshopper's."

"He will walk over your body up to your head. Then you must shake all your body. Do you understand, Pivi?"

"Yes, dear lady, I shall do just as you say."

"Very good," said the woman, going out and shutting the door.

Pivi lay still under his coverings, then a tiny noise was heard, and the Black Ant began to march over Pivi, who lay quite still. Then came the big Red Ant, skipping along his body, and then Pivi shook himself all over. He jumped up quite well again, he ran to the river, he looked into the water and saw that he was changed from a bird into a fine young man!

"Oh, lady," he cried, "look at me now! I am changed into a man, and so handsome!"

"Will you obey me again?" said the woman.

"Always; whatever you command, I will do it," said Pivi politely.

"Then climb up that cocoa-nut tree, with your legs only, not using your hands," said the woman.

Now the natives can run up cocoa-nut trees like squirrels, some using only one hand; the girls can do that. But few can climb without using their hands at all.

"At the top of the tree you will find two cocoa-nuts. You must not throw them down, but carry them in your hands; and you must descend as you went up, using your legs only."

"I shall try, at least," said Pivi.

And up he went, but it was very difficult, and down he came.

"Here are your cocoa-nuts," he said, presenting them to the woman.

"Now, Pivi, put them in the shed where you lay, and when the sun sets to cool himself in the sea, and rise again not so hot in the dawn, you must go and take the nuts."

All day Pivi played about in the river, as the natives do, throwing fruit and silvery showers of water at each other. When the sun set he went into the hut. But as he drew near he heard sweet voices talking and laughing within.

"What is that? People chattering in the hut! Perhaps they have taken my cocoa-nuts," said Pivi to himself.

In he went, and there he found two pretty, laughing, teasing girls. He hunted for his cocoa-nuts, but none were there.

Down he ran to the river.

"Oh, lady, my nuts have been stolen!" he cried.

"Come with me, Pivi, and there will be nuts for you," said the woman.

They went back to the hut where the girls were laughing and playing.

"Nuts for you?" said the woman. "There are two wives for you, Pivi, take them to your house."

"Oh, good lady," cried Pivi, "how kind you are!"

So they were married and very happy, when in came cross old Kabo.

"Is this Pivi?" said he. "Yes, it is—no, it isn't. It is not the same Pivi—but there is a kind of likeness. Tell me, *are* you Pivi?"

"Oh, yes," said Pivi. "But I am much better-looking, and there are my two wives, are they not beautiful?"

"You are mocking me, Pivi! Your wives? How? Where did you get them? *You*, with wives!"

Then Pivi told Kabo about the kind woman, and all the wonderful things that had happened to him.

"Well, well!" said Kabo, "but I want to be handsome too, and to have pretty young wives."

"But how can we manage that?" asked Pivi.

"Oh, we shall do all the same things over again—play at slinging, and this time you shall break my leg, Pivi!"

"With all the pleasure in life," said Pivi, who was always ready to oblige.

So they went slinging, and Pivi broke Kabo's leg, and Kabo fell into the river, and floated into the bamboo, and the woman blew him out, just as before. Then she picked up Kabo, and put him in the shed and told him what to do when the Black Ant came, and what to do when the Red Ant came. But he didn't!

When the Black Ant came, he shook himself, and behold, he had a twisted leg, and a hump back, and was as black as the ant.

Then he ran to the woman.

"Look, what a figure I am!" he said; but she only told him to climb the tree, as she had told Pivi.

But Kabo climbed with both hands and feet, and he threw down the nuts, instead of carrying them down, and he put them in the hut. And when he went back for them there, he found two horrid old black hags, wrangling and scolding and scratching. So back he went to Pivi with his two beautiful wives, and Pivi was very sorry, but what could he do? Nothing but sit and cry.

So, one day, Kabo came and asked Pivi to sail in his canoe to a place where he knew of a great big shell-fish, enough to feed on for a week. Pivi went, and deep in the clear water they saw a monstrous shell-fish, like an oyster, as big as a rock, with the shell wide open.

"We shall catch it and dry it and kipper it," said Pivi, "and give a dinner to all our friends!"

"I shall dive for it, and break it off the rock," said Kabo, "and then you must help me to drag it up into the canoe."

There the shell-fish lay and gaped, but Kabo, though he dived in, kept well out of the way of the beast.

Up he came, puffing and blowing.

"Oh, Pivi!" he cried, "I cannot move it. Jump in and try it yourself!"

Pivi dived, with his spear, and the shell-fish opened its shell wider yet, and sucked, and Pivi disappeared into its mouth, and the shell shut up with a snap!

Kabo laughed like a fiend, and then went home.

"Where is Pivi?" asked the two pretty girls.

Kabo pretended to cry and told how Pivi had been swallowed.

"But dry your eyes, my darlings," said Kabo. "I will be your husband, and my wives shall be your slaves. Everything is for the best, in the best of all possible worlds."

"No, no!" cried the girls. "We love Pivi. We do not

love anyone else. We shall stay at home, and weep for Pivi!"

"Wretched idiots!" cried Kabo; "Pivi was a scoundrel who broke my leg, and knocked me into the water."

Then a little cough was heard at the door, and Kabo trembled, for he knew it was the cough of Pivi!

"Ah, dear Pivi!" cried Kabo, rushing to the door. "What joy! I was trying to console your dear wives."

Pivi said not one word. He waved his hand, and five and twenty of his friends came trooping down the hill. They cut up Kabo into little pieces. Pivi turned round and there was the good woman of the river.

"Pivi," she said, "how did you get out of the living tomb into which Kabo sent you?"

"I had my spear with me," said Pivi. "It was quite dry inside the shell, and I worked away at the fish with my spear, till he saw reason to open his shell and out I came."

Then the good woman laughed; and Pivi and his two wives lived happy ever afterwards.

From THE BROWN FAIRY BOOK

The Dolphin, the Nautilus and the Crocodile

PLINY THE ELDER: translated by H. RACKHAM

These pieces are from Pliny the Elder's Natural History *which was finished in the year A.D. 77.*

Pliny took a great interest in everything scientific and his book tells us what the ancient Romans knew about botany, geography, mineralogy and the workings of the human body, as well as about animals and fish. Some of the creatures he describes probably never existed at all. What I like most about them is the way he sums up their characters.

He died at the eruption of Vesuvius in A.D. 79—not because he was in Pompeii when it was smothered in ashes but because he sailed very close in to the shore to get a good look at what was happening, and breathed in some of the poisonous vapours. It was an honourable death for a scientific man.

The Dolphin

THE dolphin is an animal that is not only friendly to mankind but is also a lover of music, and it can be charmed by singing in harmony, but particularly by the sound of the water-organ. It is not afraid of a human being as something strange to it, but comes to meet vessels at sea and sports and gambols round them, actually trying to race them and passing them even when under full sail.

In the reign of the late lamented Augustus a dolphin that had been brought into the Lucrine Lake fell marvellously in love with a certain boy, a poor man's son, who used to go from the Baiae district to school at Pozzuoli, because fairly often the lad when loitering about the place at noon called to him by the name of Snubnose and coaxed him with bits of bread he had with him for the journey—I should be ashamed to tell the story were it not that it has been written by Maecenas and Fabianus and Flavius Alfius and many others—and when the boy called to it at whatever time of the day, although it was concealed in hiding it used to fly to him out of the depth, eat out of his hand, and let him mount on its back, sheathing as it were the prickles of its fin, and used to carry him when mounted right across the bay to Pozzuoli to school, bringing him back in similar manner, for several years, until the boy died of disease, and then it used to keep coming sorrowfully and like a mourner to the accustomed place, and itself also expired, quite undoubtedly from longing.

PLINY: NATURAL HISTORY

The Nautilus

BUT among outstanding marvels is the creature called the nautilus, and by others the pilot-fish. Lying on its back it comes to the surface of the sea, gradually raising itself up in such a way that by sending out all the water through a tube it so to speak unloads itself of bilge and sails easily. Afterwards it twists back its two foremost arms and spreads out between them a marvellously thin membrane, and with this serving as a sail in the breeze while it uses its other arms underneath it like oars, it steers itself with its tail between them as a rudder. So it proceeds across the deep mimicking the likeness of a fast cutter, if any alarm interrupts its voyage submerging itself by sucking in water.

PLINY: NATURAL HISTORY

The Crocodile

THIS belongs to the Nile; it is a curse on four legs, and equally pernicious on land and in the river. It is the only land animal not furnished with a tongue and the only one that bites by pressing down the mobile upper jaw, and it is also formidable because of its row of teeth set close together like a comb. In size it usually exceeds eighteen ells. It lays as many eggs as a goose, and by a kind of prophetic instinct incubates them always outside the line to which the Nile in that year is going to rise at full flood. Nor does any other animal grow to greater dimensions from a smaller original size; however it is armed with talons as well, and its hide is invincible against

all blows. It passes its days on land and its nights in the water, in both cases for reasons of warmth. This creature when sated with a meal of fish and sunk in sleep on the shore with its mouth always full of food, is tempted by a small bird (called there the trochilus but in Italy the king-bird) to open its mouth to enable the bird to feed; and first it hops in and cleans out the mouth, and then the teeth and inner throat also, which yawns open as wide as possible for the pleasure of this scratching; and the ichneumon watches for it to be overcome by sleep in the middle of this gratification and darts like a javelin through the throat so opened and gnaws out the belly.

PLINY: NATURAL HISTORY

The Grasshopper and the Ant

LA FONTAINE

The grasshopper, at song,
   All summer long,
When winter winds blew rude
Found herself short of food:
Nor did the smallest grain
Of fly or worm remain.
She went with loud complaint
To her nearest neighbour, the ant,
Beseeching her to give

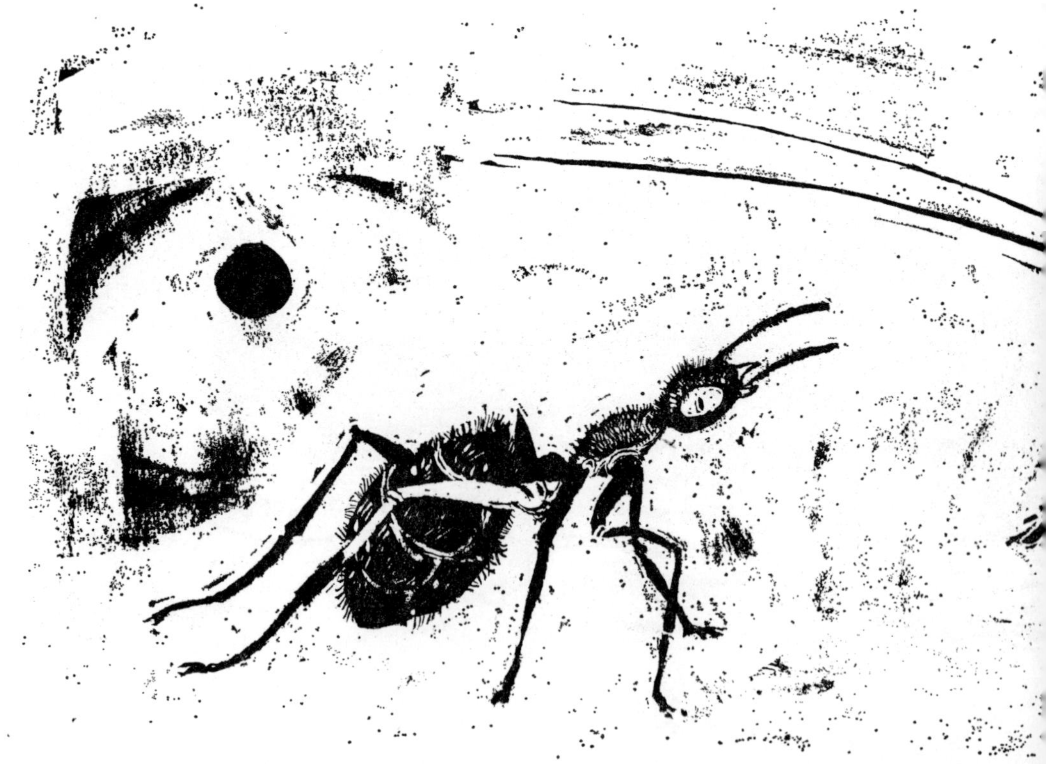

Enough to keep her alive
Till summer came once more.
—I'll pay you back, she swore,
In August, on my word as an animal,
Interest and principal.
The ant, we may safely state,
Was rarely tempted to lend.
—How was your summer spent?
She asked this borrower straight.
—Night and day, at every chance,
I sang, if I may make so free.
—You sang? That's all right by me.
Very well. Now you may dance.

Translated from the French by EILÍS DILLON

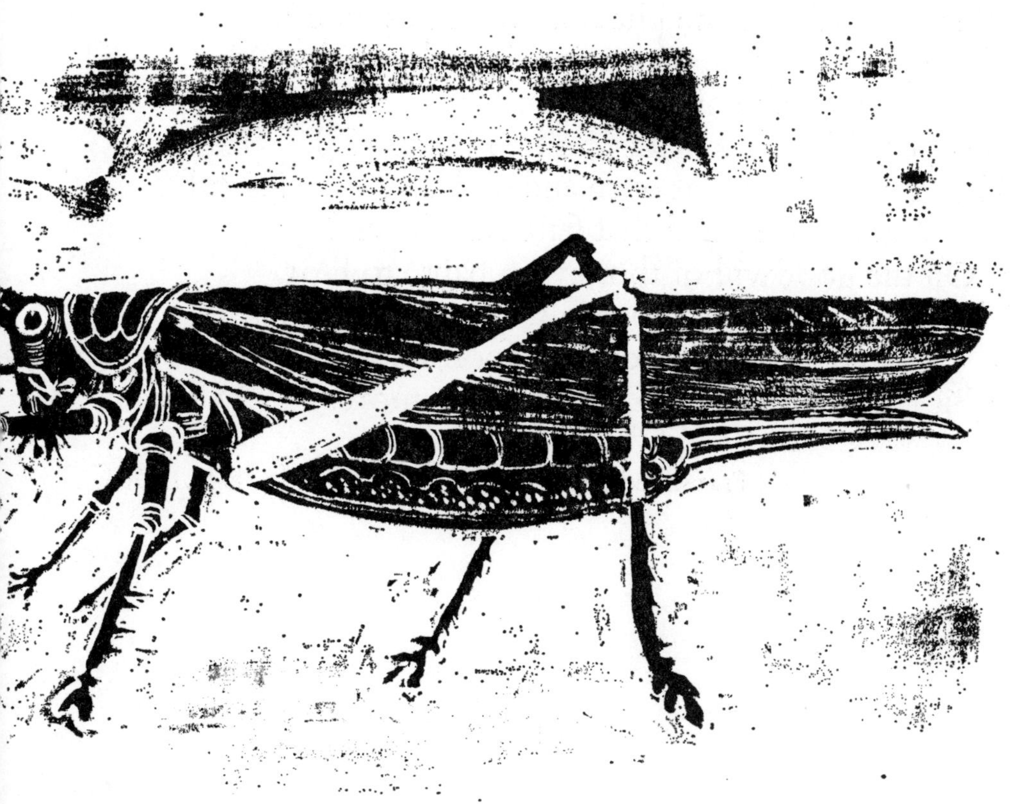

The Crow and the Fox

LA FONTAINE

Master Crow, in a tree perching,
Held in his beak a cheese.
Master Fox, on his way, smelling,
Set himself out to please:
Hi! good day to you, Mr. Crow,
You're a fine fellow! You're so handsome, I know
That if you can sing
To match your wing
We must call you the phoenix of all this wood.
These words put the Crow in a joyful mood,
And to make his sweetest call
He opened his beak wide and let his prey fall.
The Fox grabbed it at once and said: My dear Friend,
You have learned that flatterers depend
On the goodwill of those who pause to hear.
This lesson is worth a cheese, it's clear.
The Crow, ashamed of his foolishness, swore
A bit late, he'd be taken for a fool no more.

Translated from the French by EILÍS DILLON

The Lion, Of Parrots, Of Crabs

Translated and adapted by T. H. WHITE

These three pieces are taken from a Bestiary which was originally written in Latin. From the second century onwards, Christian writers drew moral lessons from the behaviour of animals, sometimes stretching the story a bit to make it sound better.

The oldest illustrated bestiary goes back to the ninth century and is in the Royal Library in Brussels but most of those that can be seen now are from the thirteenth century. I think these pieces are very like Pliny's, though their purpose was quite different.

The Lion

LEO the Lion, mightiest of beasts, will stand up to anybody.

The word 'beasts' should properly be used about lions, leopards, tigers, wolves, foxes, dogs, monkeys, and others which rage about with tooth and claw—with the exception of snakes. They are called Beasts because of the violence with which they rage, and are known as 'wild' (*ferus*) because they are accustomed to freedom by nature and are governed (*ferantur*) by their own wishes. They wander hither and thither, fancy free, and they go where-ever they want to go.

The name 'Lion' (*leo*) has been turned into Latin from a Greek root, for it is called '*leon*' in Greek—but this is a muddled name, partly corrupted, since '*leon*' has also been translated as 'king' from Greek into Latin, owing to the fact that he is the Prince of All Animals.

They say that the litters of these creatures come in threes. The short ones with curly manes are peaceful: the tall ones with plain hair are fierce.

The nature of their brows and hair-tufts is an index to their disposition. Their courage is seated in their hearts, while their constancy is in their heads. They fear the creaking of wheels, but are frightened by fire even more so.

A lion, proud in the strength of his own nature, knows not how to mingle his ferocity with all and sundry, but, like the king he is, disdains to have a lot of different wives.

Scientists say that Leo has three principal characteristics.

His first feature is that he loves to saunter on the tops of mountains. Then, if he should happen to be pursued by hunting men, the smell of the hunters reaches up to him, and he disguises his spoor behind him with his tail. Thus the sportsmen cannot track him.

It was in this way that our Saviour (i.e. the Spiritual Lion of the Tribe of Judah, the Rod of Jesse, the Lord of Lords, the Son of God) once hid the spoor of his love in the high places, until, being sent by the Father, he came down into the womb of the virgin Mary and saved the human race which had perished. Ignorant of the fact that his spoor could be concealed, the Devil (i.e. the hunter of humankind) dared to pursue him with temptations like a mere man. Even the angels themselves who were on high, not recognising his spoor, said to those who were going up with him when he ascended to his reward: "Who is this King of Glory?"

The Lion's second feature is, that when he sleeps, he seems to keep his eyes open.

In this very way, Our Lord also, while sleeping in the body, was buried after being crucified—yet his Godhead was awake. As it is said in the *Song of Songs*, "I am asleep and my heart is awake", or, in the Psalm, "Behold, he that keepeth Israel shall neither slumber nor sleep."

The third feature is this, that when a lioness gives birth to her cubs, she brings them forth dead and lays them up lifeless for three days—until their father, coming on the third day, breathes in their faces and makes them alive.

Just so did the Father Omnipotent raise Our Lord Jesus Christ from the dead on the third day. Quoth Jacob: "He shall sleep like a lion, and the lion's whelp shall be raised."

So far as their relations with men are concerned, the nature of lions is that they do not get angry unless they are wounded.

Any decent human ought to pay attention to this. For men do get angry when they are not wounded, and they oppress the innocent although the law of Christ bids them to let even the guilty go free.

The compassion of lions, on the contrary, is clear from innumerable examples—for they spare the prostrate; they allow such captives as they come across to go back to their own country; they prey on men rather than on women, and they do not kill children except when they are very hungry.

Furthermore, lions abstain from over-eating: in the first place because they only take food and drink on alternate days—and frequently, if digestion has not followed, they are even in the habit of putting off the day for dinner. In the second place, they pop their paws carefully into their mouths and pull out the meat of their own accord, when they have eaten too much. Indeed, if they have to run away from somebody, they perform the same action if they are full up.

Lack of teeth is a sign of old age in lions.

From THE BOOK OF BEASTS

Of Parrots

IT is only from India that one can get a Psitiacus or Parrot, which is a green bird with a red collar and a large tongue. The tongue is broader than in other birds and it makes distinct sounds with it. If you did not see it, you would think it was a real man talking. It greets people of its own accord, saying "What-cheer?" or "Toodle-oo!" It learns other words by teaching. Hence the story of the man who paid a compliment to Caesar by giving him a parrot which had been taught to say: "I, a parrot, am willing to learn the names of others from you. This I learnt by myself to say—Hail Caesar!"

A parrot's beak is so hard that if you throw down the bird from a height on a rock, it saves itself by landing on its beak with its mouth tight shut, using the beak as a kind of foundation for the shock. Actually its whole skull is so thick that, if it has to be taught anything, it needs to be admonished with blows. Although it really does try to copy what its teacher is saying, it wants an occasional crack with an iron bar. While young, and up to two years old, it learns what you point out to it quickly enough, and retains it tenaciously; but after that it begins to be distrait and unteachable.

From THE BOOK OF BEASTS

Of Crabs

CANCER the Crab goes in for a cunning stratagem, due to his greed. He is very fond of oysters and likes to get himself a banquet of their flesh. But although eager for dinner, he understands the danger, since the pursuit is as difficult as it is hazardous. It is difficult because the inner flesh of the oyster is contained within very strong shells, as if nature its maker had by her imperial command fortified the soft part of the body with walls. She feeds and cherishes this flesh in a kind of arched dome in the middle of the shell; disposes it, as it were, in a sort of hollow. For this reason, the handling of oysters has to be done carefully; because nothing can open the closed oyster by force, and thus it is dangerous for the crab to insert his claw. Betaking himself to artfulness, therefore, the crab lays an ambush with a new plot of his own. Because all species delight in relaxing themselves, the crab investigates to find out whether at any time the oyster opens that double shell of his in places remote from all wind and safe from the rays of the sun, or whether it unlocks the fastenings of its gates, so that it may pleasure its internal organs in the free air. Then the crab, secretly casting in a pebble, prevents the closing of the oyster, and thus, finding the lock forced, inserts his claws safely and feeds on the internal flesh.

Now is that not just like men—those corrupt creatures who follow the habit of the crab, creep into the practice of unnatural trickery and eke out the weakness of their real powers by a sort of cunning. They join deceit to cruelty and are fed upon the distress of others. Do you, therefore, be content with your own things and do not seek the injury of your neighbours to support you.

The simple fare of a man who does no harm is the right food. Having his own property he knows not how to plot against his fellow man's, nor does he burn with flames of avarice. Covetousness is to him only a loss of virtue and an incentive to greed. And so, blessed is that poverty which truthfully sticks to its own goods, and meet it is to be preferred above all riches. "Better a little with the fear of the

Lord than great treasure and trouble therewith: better is a dinner of herbs where love is, than a stalled ox and hatred therewith."

Let us then devote ourselves to acquiring merit and to maintaining what is wholesome, not to the cheating of another's innocence. Let it be left to us to make use of the marine example in perfecting our well-being, not in the undoing of our neighbour.

From THE BOOK OF BEASTS

The Ant and the Sluggard

Go to the ant, thou sluggard; consider her ways and be wise:
Which having no guide, overseer or ruler,
Provideth her meat in the summer, and gathereth her food in the harvest.
How long wilt thou sleep, O sluggard? when wilt thou arise out of thy sleep?
Yet a little sleep, a little slumber, a little folding of the hands to sleep:
So shall thy poverty come as one that travelleth, and thy want as an armed man.

PROVERBS vi, 6–11

Odysseus and Argus

HOMER: translated by E. V. RIEU

Odysseus was the son of Laertes, king of Ithaca in Greece. His wife was Penelope and he had a son called Telemachus. Odysseus went to the wars, but as he was about to start for home he was blown off course by a fierce storm and this began a series of terrible adventures. He managed to land on various islands but each time he barely escaped with his life, and at last after many years he reached home again.

Disguised as a beggar he went to his own house where his wife Penelope was waiting anxiously for his return. The story tells how she refused to marry anyone else, though she was pressed very hard, until she would have finished the web she was weaving. She never did finish it, because when everyone had gone to bed at night, she always got up and ripped out the work she had done during the day. At last her patience and devotion were rewarded.

ODYSSEUS and his trusty swineherd had arrived; but they paused for a moment outside when the notes from a well-made lyre came to their ears. For Phemius was just preparing to give the company a song.

"Eumaeus," said Odysseus taking the swineherd by the arm, "this must surely be Odysseus' palace: it would be easy to pick it out at a glance from any number of houses. There are buildings beyond buildings; the courtyard wall with its battlements is a fine piece of work and those folding doors are true defences. No one could afford to turn up his nose at this. I gather too that a large company is there for dinner: one can smell the roast, and someone is playing the lyre. Music and banquets always go together."

"You have made no mistake," said Eumaeus, "but you are naturally observant. Let us consider our next move. Either you go into the palace first and approach the Suitors, while I stay where I am; or if you prefer it, you wait here and let me be the first to go in. But in that case don't be long, or they may see you here outside and take a shot at you or beat you off. I leave it to you to decide."

"And rightly too," said the stalwart Odysseus, "for I understand the position. You shall go in first while I stay here, for I am quite used to blows and missiles. I have been toughened by what I have suffered in the field and on the sea. After all that, what matters a bit more? But if there is anything that a man can't conceal it is a ravening belly—that utter curse, the cause of so much trouble to mankind, which even prompts them to fit out great ships and sail the barren seas, bringing death and destruction to their enemies."

Stretched on the ground close to where they stood talking, there lay a dog, who now pricked up his ears and raised his head. Argus was his name. Odysseus himself had owned and trained him, though he had sailed for holy Ilium before he could reap the reward of his patience. In years gone by the young huntsmen had often taken him out after wild goats, deer and hares. But now, in his owner's absence, he lay abandoned on the heaps of dung from the mules and cattle which lay in profusion at the gate, awaiting removal by Odysseus' servants as manure for his great estate. There, full of vermin, lay Argus the hound. But directly he became aware of Odysseus' presence, he wagged his tail and dropped his ears, though he lacked the strength now to come any nearer to his master. Yet

Odysseus saw him out of the corner of his eye, and brushed a tear away without showing any sign of emotion to the swineherd, whom he now proceeded to sound:

"Eumaeus, it is very odd to see a hound like this lying in the dung. He's a beauty, though one cannot really tell whether his looks were matched by his pace, or whether he was just one of those dogs whom their masters feed at table and keep for show."

"It's plain enough," said the swineherd Eumaeus, "that this is a dog whose master has met his death abroad. If you could see him in the heyday of his looks and form, as Odysseus left him when he sailed for Troy, you'd be astonished by his speed and power. No game that he gave chase to could escape him in the forest glades. For beside all else he was a marvel at picking up the scent. But now he's in a bad way; his master far away from home has come to grief, and the women are too careless to groom him. Servants, when their masters are no longer there to order them about, have little will to do their duties as they should. All-seeing Zeus takes half the good out of a man on the day when he becomes a slave."

With this Eumaeus left him, entered the great house and passed straight into the hall where the young gallants were assembled. As for Argus, he had no sooner set eyes on Odysseus after those nineteen years than he succumbed to the black hand of Death.

From THE ODYSSEY

Chanticleer and Pertelote

GEOFFREY CHAUCER: prose version by EILÍS DILLON

ONCE, a long time ago, a poor old widow lived in a small cottage in a valley. She had only one little field, as well as a piece of woodland, and since the death of her husband she had lived in great poverty. Still she did not complain, and she and her two daughters made the best they could of their tiny farm. By using every inch of it they managed to keep three sows, three cows and a sheep named Molly.

You may be sure that there was not much luxury in that house, nor even time to keep it clean and tidy. The widow and her daughters had to work so hard that everything they ate at dinner tasted good. As the mother said, they were sure of being healthy since the whole world knows that overeating is the most common cause of sickness, drinking wine causes apoplexy and gout, and they were even spared the worry of being in debt since no one in their senses would give them credit. They lived on the things they grew, milk and bacon and eggs, with brown bread in plenty, the healthiest diet possible.

Beside the house there was a poultry-yard with a stockade all around it, and a dry ditch beyond that. In this yard the widow kept a cock called Chanticleer, famous for his great crowing which everyone said was more cheerful even than the sound of the organ in the church. More extraordinary still, he always crowed exactly at dawn, though as we all know the dawn comes a little later every day as the year goes on to the summer. You could depend on that cock, more than you could depend on the bells of the church, and what more can one say in his praise? His comb was as red as the very best coral, battlemented like a castle wall. His bill was black and shiny like jet, his legs were blue and so were his toes, while his nails were as white as a lily. His feathers were like polished gold. A fine sight, was that cock.

There were seven hens in the poultry-yard, as beautifully coloured as the cock, but the most beautiful of all was Pertelote. She was a polite, discreet, cheerful, friendly hen always on her best behaviour. Since she was seven days old Chanticleer had been in love with her, and she with him. When the sun rose in the morning he addressed his first song to her, and the words were: "My love is far from land"—for of course at that time, long, long ago, all the birds and animals could speak and sing as we do.

One morning, just at dawn, when Chanticleer and Pertelote and all the other hens were on their perch in the widow's kitchen, with Pertelote, naturally, next to Chanticleer, he began to groan and lurch like someone having a bad dream. Pertelote, hearing him scream, was very frightened and said:

"O dearest love, what's the matter with you? Why are you groaning and shaking? You should be asleep at this hour—you're waking everyone up with your noise."

"I'm sorry about that," said Chanticleer, "but I can't help it. Just now I had such an awful dream, I can still feel my heart thumping. Since dreams go by opposites, I hope God will make that one a sign of good to us all and keep me safe. I dreamed that I was rambling around our yard when I saw a strange animal, a sort of a dog, that made a grab at me, meaning to kill me! His fur was a reddish yellow, with dark tips to his ears and his tail; a thoroughly nasty specimen. His nose was small, and he had burning, bright eyes that would frighten the very life out of you. That's why I was groaning and moaning just now, in my sleep."

"You ought to be ashamed of yourself!" said Pertelote. "Such a coward! Now I can never love you again. How could I love a coward? What every woman wants is a tough, reliable, independent, crafty, discreet, generous, wise husband, not one that boasts and then has no courage when the time comes for it. How could you dare to tell me, your loving wife, that you're afraid of anything? A grown man should have the courage of a man—how can a mere dream frighten you so much? We all know there's no truth in dreams, that they only come from eating too much, wind in the stomach, indigestion. That's what made you dream red—too much red blood in you. People always dream red after eating rich food—bloody arrows, red fires, big red dragons waiting to fight them, big red dogs with little red pups at their heels to bite them."

All this happened on the third of May. Later in the morning, Chanticleer and his seven wives were walking in the yard under the blazing sun. At nine o'clock, the cock was suddenly inspired to call their attention to the beauty of the day with a triumphant crow:

"Look at the sun! The sun is up, my seven! Look, it has climbed forty degrees—in fact while I was calling you it climbed one more, and that makes forty-one degrees. My nature as a cock tells me all about it. Dear Madam Pertelote, my love, just listen to those happy birds singing! Look at the flowers, growing so beautifully! O I feel so happy!"

But as often happens in this sad world, just then Fate had a nasty surprise in store for him. All the wisest men agree that earthly joys never last long and as this story is perfectly true, I must tell it though it is sad.

A sly wicked fox, with ears and tail tipped black as coal, had been lurking around the wood for three long years, and that very night he had managed at last to get through into the farmyard where Chanticleer and all his ladies used to walk. Now he lay still in a bed of cabbages, watching the cock and waiting his chance, like the little murderer he was. Chanticleer had been warned by his dream that this would be a bad day for him, but what was fated to be had to happen. That is the way of the world, as all the great philosophers tell us. In fact if his wife had not laughed at him for being a coward, Chanticleer might have taken more notice of that dream and got off better. And that is how women are, from Adam down to the present day—that is not my view but Chanticleer's. I think very well of all women.

So there was Pertelote taking a dust-bath in the sand, with the other hens all around her basking in the sun, and Chanticleer, very pleased with himself, was letting his voice out good and loud. As it happened, he saw a butterfly flutter past and followed it with his eye to where it landed, on the cabbage where the fox was hiding. Poor Chanticleer got a bad fright, though he had never seen a fox before in all his life.

"Cok, cok," said he, spoiling his song, and half turned to gallop away.

Quickly the fox said:

"Sir, where are you off to? Surely you're not afraid of me? I'm a friend of yours—how can I do you any harm? You may even have thought I was spying on you, seeing

me lying here so quiet and so well hidden, but what I'm really here for is to listen to your wonderful voice. That's what I came for, knowing that you have a voice like an angel and a knowledge of music to match it. Both your father and your mother visited me at my house, to my great pleasure, and I'd be very glad to see you there too. As surely as I hope for heaven, your father was the best singer I ever heard announce the dawn of day. It welled up from his soul, and he had such splendid control! He always sang with his eyes shut, and strutted along on the tips of his toes, with his neck stretched out and his delicate beak wide open, so that everyone watching him was impressed with his skill. I've heard tell of other famous cocks but I can't believe they could be as fine as your father. I implore you, in memory of him, to sing your best now for me!"

Chanticleer was so flattered with all this that he had no room in his mind for doubts about the fox's honesty. He flapped his wings, stood high on his toes, stretched his neck and opened his beak, and shutting his eyes tight he began to sing as loudly as he could. The fox waited for no more, but grabbed him by the throat, flung him all along his back and carried him off towards the woods, the brute, unseen by anyone who might have prevented him.

Poor Chanticleer! If only he had stayed up on his perch that day, and if only his wife had paid heed to his dream! In a moment, all his ladies were yelling their heads off and Pertelote was the loudest of all, louder than the yells of the women of Troy or ancient Rome when they saw disaster fall on their houses. Hearing all the clamour, the widow and her two daughters came running out of the house and were just in time to see the fox streaking off to his covert with Chanticleer stretched flat on his shoulder.

"Look, look!" they cried. "O mercy, look at that! Ha! Ha! The fox!"

And they all ran after him.

Every man working in the fields around grabbed his stick and called his dog and ran after them too. Our dog Coll was one of them, and the neighbours' dogs, Talbot and Bran and Shaggy, and out of the next house where she had been spinning, fat Maggie ran, brandishing her distaff in her hand. The cow and the calf and the pigs ran, terrified at the barking of the dogs, and all the men and women were shouting and making a fearful noise and hardly able to breathe with the speed of the chase and with their yells. The ducks flew out of the water, quacking and flapping as if their necks were being wrung, and the geese took fright and flew up into the trees. The bees came swarming out of the hive, to add their bit to the confusion, and some of the people carried horns and trumpets which they blew as loudly as they could, so that you would think the sky would fall.

The cock, though he was in a sorry state lying on the fox's back, managed to gather his wits enough to say:

"Sir Fox, if I were you I'd turn on that pack of country clowns and shout: 'Turn back, you impertinent yokels! May you all die of the plague! Now that I've reached the wood safely, no matter what you do, the cock is mine for good. I'll eat him there in my own good time!' "

The fox answered:

"That's exactly what I'll do!"

But when he opened his mouth to speak, the cock smartly broke away from him and flew out of his reach into the high branches of a tree.

Seeing what had happened, the fox said:

"O my poor Chanticleer, I'm afraid I must have frightened you. I grabbed you too hard when I caught hold of you. But Sir, I meant no harm. Please don't be offended: just come down and I'll explain what I meant by it."

"No," said the cock. "We're a sorry pair but I'd be the worse of the two if I were to let you take me in more than once. You made a nice fool of me, asking me to shut my eyes and sing for you—I won't let that happen to me again. Anyone that shuts his eyes when he should keep them open doesn't deserve to live at all."

"If you ask me," said the fox, "the biggest fool is the one who chatters when he should hold his tongue."

The Singing Masons

Therefore doth heaven divide
The state of man in divers functions,
Setting endeavour in continual motion;
To which is fixed as an aim or butt
Obedience; for so work the honey bees,
Creatures that by a rule in nature teach
The act of order to a peopled kingdom.
They have a king, and officers of sorts,
Where some like magistrates correct at home;
Others like merchants venture trade abroad;
Others like soldiers armed in their stings,
Make boot upon the summer's velvet buds,
Which pillage they with merry march bring home
To the tent-royal of their emperor;
Who, busied in his majesty, surveys
The singing masons building roofs of gold,
The civil citizens kneading up the honey,
The poor mechanic porters crowding in
Their heavy burdens at his narrow gate,
The sad-eyed justice, with his surly hum,
Delivering o'er to executors pale
The lazy yawning drone. I this infer,
That many things, having full reference
To one consent, may work contrariously;
As many arrows loosed several ways
Come to one mark.

WILLIAM SHAKESPEARE — *From* KING HENRY V

Cock-Alu and Hen-Alie

MARY HOWITT

COCK-ALU and Hen-Alie sat on the perch above the bean-straw. It was four o'clock in the morning, and Cock-Alu clapped his wings and crowed; then, turning to Hen-Alie he said:

"Hen-Alie, my little wife, I love you better than all the world; you know I do. I always told you so! I will do anything for you; I'll go round the world for you; I'll travel as far as the sun for you! You know I would! Tell me, what shall I do for you?"

"Crow!" said Hen-Alie.

"Oh, that is such a little thing!" said Cock-Alu, and crowed with all his might.

He crowed so loud that he woke the farmer's wife, and the dog and the cat and all the pigeons and horses in the stable, and the cow in the byre. He crowed so loud that all the neighbours' cocks heard him and they answered him, and they woke all their people; and thus Cock-Alu woke the whole parish.

"I've done it rarely this morning!" said Cock-Alu. "I told you I would do anything to please you!"

The next morning, at breakfast, as Hen-Alie was picking the beans out of the beanstraw, one stuck in her throat, and she was soon so ill that she was ready to die.

"Oh, Cock-Alu," said she, calling to him in the yard where he stood clapping his wings in the sunshine, "run and fetch me a drop of dew from the silver-spring in the Beech-wood! Fetch me a drop quickly, while the dew is in it, for that is the true remedy."

But Cock-Alu was so busy crowing against a neighbour that he took no notice.

"Oh, Cock-Alu, do run and fetch me the water from the silver-spring or I shall die; for the bean sticks in my throat and nothing but water with dew in it can cure me! Oh, Cock-Alu dear, run quickly!"

Cock-Alu heard her this time and set off, crowing as he went. He had not gone far before he met the snail.

"Where are you going, snail?" says he.

"I'm going to the cow-cabbage," says the snail, "and what urgent business may it be that takes you out thus early, Cock-Alu?" says the snail.

"I'm going to the silver-spring in the Beech-wood, to fetch a drop of water for my wife Hen-Alie, who has got a bean in her throat," says Cock-Alu.

"Oh," says the snail, "run along quickly and get the water while the dew is in it; for nothing else will get a bean out of the throat. Don't stop by the way, for the bull is coming down to the silver spring to drink, and he will trouble the water. Gather up my silver-trail, however, and give it to Hen-Alie with my love, and I hope she'll soon be better."

Cock-Alu hastily gathered up the silver-trail which the snail left.

"This will make Hen-Alie a pair of stockings," said he, and went on his way.

He had not gone far before he met a wood-pigeon.

"Good morning, pigeon," says he, "and which way are you going?"

"I am going to the pea-field," says the pigeon, "to get

peas for my young ones; and what may your business be this morning, Cock-Alu?"

"I'm going to the silver-spring in the Beech-wood, to fetch a drop of water for my wife Hen-Alie, who has got a bean in her throat."

"I'm sorry to hear that," says the pigeon, "but don't let me detain you, for water with the dew in it is the best thing to get a bean out of the throat; and let me advise you to make haste, for the bloodhound is going to lap at the spring, and he will trouble the water. So run along, and here, take with you my blue velvet neck-ribbon, and give it to Hen-Alie with my love, and I hope she'll soon be better."

"Oh, what a nice pair of garters this will make for Hen-Alie!" exclaimed Cock-Alu and went on his way.

He had not gone far before he met the wild-cat.

"Good morning, friend," says Cock-Alu; "and where may you be going this morning?"

"I'm going to get a young wood-pigeon for my breakfast, while the mother is gone to the pea-field," says the wild-cat; "and where may you be travelling to this morning, Cock-Alu?"

"I'm going to the silver-spring in the Beech-wood," replied Cock-Alu, "to get a drop of water for my little wife Hen-Alie, who has got a bean in her throat."

"That's a bad business," says the wild-cat, "but a drop of water with the dew in it is the right remedy; so don't let me keep you; and you had better make haste, for the woodman is on his way to fell a tree by the spring, and if a branch falls into it, the water will be troubled; so off with you! but carry with you a flash of green fire from my right eye, and give it to Hen-Alie with my love, and I hope she'll soon be better."

"Oh, what beautiful green light, like the green on my best tail-feathers! I'll keep it for myself; it's fitter for me than for Hen-Alie!" said Cock-Alu.

So he hung the green light on his tail-feathers, which made them very handsome, and he went on his way.

He had not gone far before he met the sheep-dog.

"Good morning, sheep-dog," says Cock-Alu. "Where are you going?"

"I'm going to hunt up a stray lamb for my master," says the sheep-dog; "and what brings you abroad?"

"I'm going to the silver-spring in the Beech-wood, to get a little drop of water for my little wife Hen-Alie, who has got a bean in her throat," says Cock-Alu.

"Then why do you stop talking to me?" says the sheep-dog in his short way. "Your wife's bad enough, I'll warrant me, and a drop of water with the dew in it is the thing to do her good. Be off with you! The farmer is coming to lay the spring dry this morning; I left him sharpening his mattock when I set out. You'll be too late, if you don't mind!"

And with that the sheep-dog went his way.

"An unmannerly fellow!" says Cock-Alu, and stood looking after him. "I'll not go at his bidding, not I!" So he clapped his wings and crowed in the wood, just to show that he set light by the dog's advice. "And never to give me anything for poor little Hen-Alie, that lies sick at home with a bean in her throat! The ill-natured churl!" cried Cock-Alu to himself, and then he stood and crowed again with all his might.

After that he marched on, and before long reached the Beech-wood, but as the silver-spring lay yet a good way off, he had not gone far in the wood before he met the squirrel.

"Good morning, squirrel," says he; "what brings you abroad so early?"

"Early, do you call it, Cock-Alu?" says the squirrel. "Why, I've been up these four hours. I just stopped at the silver-spring for a drop of water while the dew was in it for my poor old husband, who lies sick a-bed. I'm now on my way back again, for there is nothing like water with dew in it; I've got it here in a cherry-leaf. And pray you, what business may take you abroad, Cock-Alu?"

"The same as yours," replied Cock-Alu. "I'm going for water too, for my wife Hen-Alie, who has got a bean in her throat."

"Ah, well-a-day," says the squirrel, "that's a bad thing! But run along with you, for the old sow is coming down with her nine little pigs, and if they trouble the water it will be all too late for poor little Hen-Alie!"

And with that the squirrel leaped up into the oak-tree above where Cock-Alu stood, for that was her way home, and left him without further ceremony.

"Humph!" said Cock-Alu; "she might have given me some of the water out of her cherry-leaf for my poor little Hen-Alie!"

And so saying he walked on through the Beech-wood, and as he met no more creatures he soon reached the silver-spring.

But it was now noon-day, and there was not a drop of dew in the water, and the bull had been down and drunk, and the blood-hound had lapped, and the old sow and her nine little pigs had wallowed in it, so the water was troubled, and besides that the woodman had felled the tree, which now lay across the spring, and the farmer was digging the new watercourse, so the spring was getting lower every minute. Cock-Alu had come quite too late; there was not a drop left for poor little Hen-Alie.

When Cock-Alu saw this he was very much disconcerted; he did not know what to do. He stood a little while considering, and then he set off as hard as he could for the squirrel's house to beg a drop of water from her. But the squirrel lived a long way off in the wood, and thus it was a considerable time before he got there.

When he reached the squirrel's house, however, nobody was at home. He knocked and knocked for a long time, and at last he walked in, but they were all gone out. He peeped, therefore, into the pantry to see if he could find the water. There were plenty of hazel-nuts and beech-nuts—heaps and heaps of them, all laid up in store for winter—but no water. At length he saw the curled-up cherry-leaf, like a water-jug, standing at the squirrel's bedside; but it was empty; there was not a single drop in it.

"This is a bad business!" said Cock-Alu to himself, and turned to leave the house.

At the squirrel's door he met the woodpecker.

"Woodpecker," says he, "where is the squirrel gone to? I want to beg a drop of water from the silver-spring for my wife Hen-Alie, who has got a bean in her throat."

"Lack-a-day!" said the woodpecker, "the old squirrel drank every drop, and drained the jug into the bargain. He lay sick in bed this morning, but there was such virtue in the water that he got well as soon as he drank it, and now he has taken his wife and the little ones out for an airing. They will not be back till night, I know. But if you will leave any message with me I will be sure to deliver it, for the squirrel and I are very neighbourly."

"Oh!" groaned Cock-Alu; "but what would be the use of leaving a message if they have no water to give me?"

With that he came down from the old pine-tree where the squirrel lived, set out on his way home again, and came at length out of the Beech-wood; but it was then getting towards evening.

He came to his own yard. There was the perch on which he and Hen-Alie had so often sat, and there was the bean-straw, and there lay poor Hen-Alie just as he had left her.

"Hen-Alie, my little wife," said he, crowing loudly as he came up, that he might put a cheerful face on the matter, "I have been very unlucky. I could not get you any water, but I have got something so nice for you! I have brought you a pair of silver-gauze stockings, which the snail has sent you, and a pair of blue velvet garters to wear with them, which the ring-dove gave me!"

"Thank you," said poor little Hen-Alie in a very weak voice, "but I wish you could have brought me some water. These things will do me no good."

"I could not bring you water, for the silver-spring is dry," said Cock-Alu, feeling very unhappy, and yet wishing to excuse himself. "There's not a drop of water left in it."

"Then it's all over with me!" sighed poor little Hen-Alie.

"Don't be down-hearted, my little wife!" said Cock-Alu, trying to seem cheerful. "I will give you something better than all. I will give you the green-fire flash from the wild-cat's right eye, which he gave me to wear on my tail-feathers. Look up, my little Hen-Alie, and I'll give it all to you."

"Alas!" sighed poor little Hen-Alie, "what good will they do me? Oh, that somebody only loved me well enough to have brought me one drop of silver-spring water!"

All this while, something very nice was happening.

There was in the poultry-yard a shabby little drab-coloured hen, very small and much despised. Cock-Alu would not look at her, nor Hen-Alie either. She had no tail-feathers at all, and long legs which looked as if she had borrowed them from a hen twice her size; she was, in short, the meanest-looking, most ill-conditioned hen in the yard.

All the time, however, that Cock-Alu was out on his fruitless errand she had been comforting Hen-Alie in the best way she could, and assuring her that Cock-Alu would soon be back again with the water from the silver-spring. But when he came back without a single drop, and only offered the fine silk stockings and blue velvet garters instead, she set off without saying a word, as fast as her long black legs would carry her, out of the wood and down to the silver-spring, which she reached in a wonderfully short time.

Fortunately the silver-spring had flowed into its new channel as clearly as ever, and the evening dew had dropped its virtues into it. The owls were shouting "Klav-vit!" from one end of the wood to the other. The dark, leathern-winged bats and the dusky white and buff-coloured moths were flitting about the broad shadows of the trees, but the little hen took no notice of any of them. On she went, thinking of nothing but what she had to do; and reaching the silver-spring she gathered up twelve drops of water, and hurrying back again, came into the yard just as poor Hen-Alie was saying:

"Oh, that somebody had loved me well enough to fetch me only one drop of silver-spring water!"

"That I do!" said the shabby little hen, and dropped one drop after another into her beak.

The first drop loosened the bean, the second softened it and the third sent it down her throat.

Hen-Alie was well again. Cock-Alu was ready to clap his wings and crow for joy and the little hen turned quietly away to her solitary perch.

"Nay," said Hen-Alie, "but you shall not go unrewarded. See, here is a pair of silk stockings for you, and here is green fire, which will make the most beautiful feathers in the world grow all over your body! Take them all, you good little thing, and to-morrow morning you will come out the handsomest hen in the yard!"

So it was. There must have been magic in those silk stockings and that green fire, for the shabby little thing was now transformed into a regular queen-hen. The farmer's wife thought she must have strayed away from some beautiful foreign country, and gave her a famous breakfast to keep her. Cock-Alu was very attentive to her; and as to Hen-Alie, she never ceased singing her praises as long as she lived.

From A WONDER BOOK OF BEASTS

The Raven

EDGAR ALLAN POE

Once upon a midnight dreary, while I pondered, weak
and weary,
Over many a quaint and curious volume of forgotten
lore—
While I nodded, nearly napping, suddenly there came a
tapping,
As of someone gently rapping, rapping at my chamber
door.
" 'Tis some visitor," I muttered, "tapping at my chamber
door—
Only this and nothing more."

Ah, distinctly I remember it was in the bleak December;
And each separate dying ember wrought its ghost upon
the floor.
Eagerly I wished the morrow; —vainly I had sought to
borrow
From my books surcease of sorrow—sorrow for the lost
Lenore—
For the rare and radiant maiden whom the angels name
Lenore—
Nameless *here* for evermore.

And the silken, sad, uncertain rustling of each purple
curtain

Thrilled me—filled me with fantastic terrors never felt
before;
So that now, to still the beating of my heart, I stood
repeating,
" 'Tis some visitor entreating entrance at my chamber
door—
Some late visitor entreating entrance at my chamber
door;—
This it is and nothing more."

Presently my soul grew stronger; hesitating then no
longer,
"Sir," said I, "or Madam, truly your forgiveness I
implore;
But the fact is I was napping, and so gently you came
rapping,
And so faintly you came tapping, tapping at my chamber
door,
That I scarce was sure I heard you"—here I opened wide
the door;—
Darkness there and nothing more.

Deep into that darkness peering, long I stood there
wondering, fearing,
Doubting, dreaming dreams no mortal ever dared to
dream before;
But the silence was unbroken, and the stillness gave no
token,
And the only word there spoken was the whispered
word, "Lenore?"
This I whispered, and an echo murmured back the word,
"Lenore!"
Merely this and nothing more.

Back into the chamber turning, all my soul within me
burning,
Soon again I heard a tapping somewhat louder than
before.
"Surely," said I, "surely that is something at my window
lattice;
Let me see, then, what thereat is, and this mystery
explore—
Let my heart be still a moment and this mystery
explore;—
'Tis the wind and nothing more!"

Open here I flung the shutter, when, with many a flirt
and flutter,
In there stepped a stately Raven of the saintly days of
yore;
Not the least obeisance made he; not a minute stopped
or stayed he;
But, with mien of lord or lady, perched above my
chamber door—
Perched upon a bust of Pallas just above my chamber
door—
Perched, and sat, and nothing more.

Then this ebony bird beguiling my sad fancy into
smiling,
By the grave and stern decorum of the countenance it
wore,
"Though thy crest be shorn and shaven, thou," I said,
"art sure no craven,
Ghastly, grim and ancient Raven wandering from the
Nightly shore—

Tell me what thy lordly name is on the Night's Plutonian shore!"
Quoth the Raven, "Nevermore."

Much I marvelled this ungainly fowl to hear discourse so plainly,
Though its answer little meaning—little relevancy bore;
For we cannot help agreeing that no living human being
Ever yet was blessed with seeing bird above his chamber door—
Bird or beast upon the sculptured bust above his chamber door,
With such name as "Nevermore."

But the Raven, sitting lonely on the placid bust, spoke only
That one word, as if his soul in that one word he did outpour.
Nothing further then he uttered—not a feather then he fluttered—
Till I scarcely more than muttered, "Other friends have flown before—
On the morrow *he* will leave me, as my hopes have flown before."
Then the bird said, "Nevermore."

Startled at the stillness broken by reply so aptly spoken,
"Doubtless," said I, "what it utters is its only stock and store
Caught from some unhappy master whom unmerciful Disaster

Followed fast and followed faster till his songs one
burden bore—
Till the dirges of his Hope that melancholy burden
bore
Of " 'Never—nevermore.' "

But the Raven still beguiling my sad fancy into smiling,
Straight I wheeled a cushioned seat in front of bird and
bust and door;
Then, upon the velvet sinking, I betook myself to
linking
Fancy unto fancy, thinking what this ominous bird of
yore—
What this grim, ungainly, ghastly, gaunt and ominous
bird of yore
Meant in croaking "Nevermore."

This I sat engaged in guessing, but no syllable expressing
To the fowl whose fiery eyes now burned into my
bosom's core;
This and more I sat divining, with my head at ease
reclining
On the cushion's velvet lining that the lamp-light gloated
o'er,
But whose velvet-violet lining with the lamp-light
gloating o'er,
She shall press, ah, nevermore!

Then, methought, the air grew denser, perfumed from
an unseen censer
Swung by seraphim whose footfalls tinkled on the
tufted floor.

"Wretch," I cried, "thy God hath lent thee—by these
 angels he hath sent thee
Respite—respite and nepenthe from thy memories of
 Lenore;
Quaff, oh, quaff this kind nepenthe and forget this lost
 Lenore!"
  Quoth the Raven, "Nevermore."

"Prophet!" said I, "thing of evil!-prophet still, if bird or
devil!—
Whether Tempter sent, or whether tempest tossed thee
here ashore,
Desolate yet all undaunted, on this desert land
enchanted—
On this home by Horror haunted—tell me truly, I
implore—
Is there—*is* there balm in Gilead? tell me—tell me, I
implore!"
Quoth the Raven, "Nevermore."

"Prophet!" said I, "thing of evil!—prophet still, if bird or
devil!
By that Heaven that bends above us—by that God we
both adore—
Tell that soul with sorrow laden if, within the distant
Aidenn,
It shall clasp a sainted maiden whom the angels name
Lenore—
Clasp a rare and radiant maiden whom the angels
name Lenore."
Quoth the Raven, "Nevermore."

"Be that word our sign of parting, bird or fiend!" I
shrieked, upstarting—
"Get thee back into the tempest and the Night's
Plutonian shore!
Leave no black plume as a token of that lie thy soul hath
spoken!
Leave my loneliness unbroken!—quit the bust above my
door!

Take thy beak from out my heart, and take thy form
from off my door!"
Quoth the Raven, "Nevermore."

And the Raven, never flitting, still is sitting, *still* is
sitting
On the pallid bust of Pallas just above my chamber
door;
And his eyes have all the seeming of a demon's that is
dreaming,
And the lamp-light o'er him streaming throws his
shadow on the floor;
And my soul from out that shadow that lies floating
on the floor
Shall be lifted—nevermore!

An Intelligent Monkey

BALDASSARE CASTIGLIONE: translated by GEORGE BULL

This piece comes from a book by Baldassare Castiglione, an Italian nobleman and soldier who lived from 1479 to 1529. The book is called The Courtier, *and was published in Venice in 1528. It was written in Urbino, at the court of the Duke, and is in the form of a conversation between different members of the court about the qualities needed in a gentleman. Sometimes they stop and tell a few stories, like this one about the ape that could play chess.*

BERNARDO said:

"What I wish to tell you is certainly not as ingenious as the last; all the same it is very fine, and it goes as follows. A few days ago the friend I have told you of was speaking about the country or world just discovered by the Portuguese mariners, and of the various animals and other things they bring back from there to

Portugal; and he claimed that he had set eyes on a monkey, of a very different kind from those we are used to seeing, which could play chess extremely well. And on one occasion, when the gentleman who had brought it was in the

presence of the King of Portugal and was playing it at chess, the monkey made some moves that were so clever as to press him hard, and eventually checkmated him.

As a result the gentleman flew into a rage (as people who lose at chess invariably do) took up the king (which being of Portuguese make was very big) and gave the monkey a great blow on the head. At once the monkey skipped aside and began to complain loudly, seeming to be demanding justice from the King himself for the wrong done to it.

The gentleman thereupon invited it to play another game, and the monkey, after a few signs of refusal, began to do so and, just as before, once again it got him into trouble. At length the monkey saw that it was in a position to give the gentleman checkmate again, and so it applied itself with fresh cunning to avoiding being struck once more. Unobtrusively, without revealing what it intended, it put its right paw under the gentleman's left elbow, which he was resting rather fastidiously on a taffeta cushion, and using its left hand to checkmate him with a pawn, having suddenly snatched the cushion away, at one and the same time it placed the cushion on its head as a shield against his blows. Then it jumped for joy in front of the King, as it celebrated its triumph. So you see how wise, wary and discreet that monkey proved to be."

Then Cesare Gonzaga remarked:

"It goes without saying that that monkey must have been a very learned member of its tribe, with great authority; and I think that the Republic of Indian Monkeys must have sent it to Portugal to win fame in a foreign land."

At this everyone laughed both at the lie that had been told and the way in which Cesare Gonzaga had added to it.

From THE BOOK OF THE COURTIER

The Nightingale

HANS CHRISTIAN ANDERSEN

IN China, you must know, the Emperor is a Chinaman, and all whom he has about him are Chinamen too. It happened a good many years ago, but that's just why it's worth while to hear the story, before it is forgotten.

The Emperor's palace was the most splendid in the world; it was made entirely of porcelain, very costly, but so delicate and brittle that one had to take care how one touched it. In the garden were to be seen the most wonderful flowers, and to the costliest of them silver bells were tied, which sounded, so that nobody should pass by without noticing the flowers. Yes, everything in the Emperor's garden was admirably arranged. And it extended so far, that even the gardener himself did not know where the end was. If a man went on and on, he came into a glorious forest with high trees and deep lakes. The wood extended straight down to the sea, which was blue and deep; great ships could sail, too, beneath the branches of the trees; and in the trees lived a Nightingale, which sang so splendidly that even the poor fisherman, who had many things to do, stopped still and listened when he had gone out at night to throw out his nets, and heard the Nightingale.

"How beautiful that is!" he said; but he was obliged to attend to his property, and thus forgot the bird. But when in the next night the bird sang again, and the fisherman heard it, he exclaimed again: "How beautiful that is!"

From all the countries of the world travellers came to the city of the Emperor, and admired it, and the palace and the garden, but when they heard the Nightingale, they said: "That is the best of all!"

And the travellers told of it when they came home; and the learned men wrote many books about the town, the palace and the garden. But they did not forget the Nightingale: that was placed highest of all; and those who were poets wrote magnificent poems about the Nightingale in the wood by the deep lake.

The books went through all the world, and a few of them once came to the Emperor. He sat in his golden chair, and read, and read: every moment he nodded his head, for it pleased him to peruse the masterly descriptions of the city, the palace and the garden. "But the Nightingale is the best of all," it stood written there.

"What's that?" exclaimed the Emperor. "I don't know the Nightingale at all! Is there such a bird in my empire and even in my garden? I've never heard of that. To think that I should have to learn such a thing for the first time from books!"

And hereupon he called his cavalier. This cavalier was so grand that if anyone lower in rank than himself dared to speak to him, or to ask him any questions, he answered nothing but "P!"—and that meant nothing.

"There is said to be a wonderful bird called a Nightingale," said the Emperor. "They say it is the best thing in all my empire. Why have I never heard anything about it?"

"I have never heard him named," replied the cavalier. "He has never been introduced at court."

"I command that he shall appear this evening, and sing before me," said the Emperor. "All the world knows what I possess, and I do not know it myself!"

"I have never heard him mentioned," said the cavalier. "I will seek for him. I will find him."

But where was he to be found? The cavalier ran up and down all the staircases, through halls and passages, but no one among all those whom he met had heard talk of the Nightingale. And the cavalier ran back to the Emperor, and said that it must be a fable invented by the writers of books.

"Your Imperial Majesty cannot believe how much is written that is fiction, besides something that they call the black art."

"But the book in which I read this," said the Emperor, "was sent to me by the high and mighty Emperor of Japan, and therefore it cannot be falsehood. I will hear the Nightingale! It must be here this evening! It has my imperial favour; and if it does not come, all the Court shall be trampled upon after the court has supped!"

"Tsing-pe!" said the cavalier; and again he ran up and down all the staircases, through halls and corridors; and half the Court ran with him, for the Courtiers did not like being trampled upon.

Then there was a great inquiry after the wonderful Nightingale, which all the world knew excepting the people at Court.

At last they met with a poor little girl in the kitchen, who said:

"The Nightingale? I know it well; yes, it can sing gloriously. Every evening I get leave to carry my poor sick mother the scraps from the table. She lives down by the strand; and when I get back and am tired, and rest in the wood, then I hear the Nightingale sing. And then the water comes into my eyes, and it is just as if my mother kissed me."

"Little kitchen girl," said the cavalier, "I will get you a place in the kitchen, with permission to see the Emperor dine, if you will but lead us to the Nightingale, for it is announced for this evening."

So they all went out into the wood where the Nightingale was accustomed to sing; half the Court went forth. When they were in the midst of their journey a cow began to low.

"Oh!" cried the Court pages, "now we have it! That shows a wonderful power in so small a creature! I have certainly heard it before."

"No, those are cows lowing," said the little kitchen girl. "We are a long way from the place yet."

Now the frogs began to croak in the marsh.

"Glorious!" said the Chinese Court preacher. "Now I hear it—it sounds just like little church bells."

"No, those are frogs," said the little kitchenmaid. "But now I think we shall soon hear it."

And then the Nightingale began to sing.

"That is it!" exclaimed the little girl. "Listen, listen! And yonder it sits."

And she pointed to a little grey bird up in the boughs.

"Is it possible?" cried the cavalier. "I should never have thought it looked like that! How simple it looks! It must certainly have lost its colour at seeing such grand people around."

"Little Nightingale!" called the little kitchenmaid, quite loudly, "our gracious Emperor wishes you to sing before him."

"With the greatest pleasure," replied the Nightingale, and began to sing most delightfully.

"It sounds just like glass bells!" said the cavalier. "And look at its little throat, how it's working! It's wonderful that we should never have heard it before. That bird will be a great success at Court."

"Shall I sing once more before the Emperor?" inquired the Nightingale, for it thought the Emperor was present.

"My excellent little Nightingale," said the cavalier, "I have great pleasure in inviting you to a Court festival this evening, when you shall charm his Imperial Majesty with your beautiful singing."

"My song sounds best in the green wood," replied the Nightingale; still it came willingly when it heard what the Emperor wished.

The palace was festively adorned. The walls and the flooring, which were of porcelain, gleamed in the rays of thousands of golden lamps. The most glorious flowers, which could ring clearly, were placed in the passages. There was a running to and fro, and a thorough draught, and all the bells rang so loudly that one could not hear oneself speak.

In the midst of the great hall, where the Emperor sat, a golden perch had been placed, on which the Nightingale was to sit. The whole Court was there, and the little cook-maid had got leave to stand behind the door, as she had now received the title of a real Court cook. All were in full dress, and all looked at the little grey bird, to whom the Emperor nodded.

And the Nightingale sang so gloriously that the tears came into the Emperor's eyes, and the tears ran down over his cheeks; then the Nightingale sang still more sweetly, that went straight to the heart. The Emperor was so much pleased that he said the Nightingale should have his golden slipper to wear round its neck. But the Nightingale declined this with thanks, saying it had already received a sufficient reward.

"I have seen tears in the Emperor's eyes—that is the real treasure to me. An Emperor's tears have a peculiar power. I am rewarded enough!"

And then it sang again with a sweet, glorious voice.

"That's the most amiable coquetry I ever saw!" said the ladies who stood round about, and then they took water in their mouths to gurgle when anyone spoke to them. They thought they should be nightingales too. And the lackeys and the chambermaids reported that they were satisfied also; and that was saying a good deal, for they are the most difficult to please. In short, the Nightingale achieved a real success.

It was now to remain at Court, to have its own cage, with liberty to go out twice every day and once at night. Twelve servants were appointed when the Nightingale went out, each of whom had a silken string fastened to the bird's legs, which they held very tight. There was really no pleasure in an excursion of that kind.

The whole city spoke of the wonderful bird, and whenever two people met, one said nothing but "Nightin," and the other said "gale"; and then they both sighed, and understood one another. Eleven pedlars' children were named after the bird, but not one of them could sing a note.

One day the Emperor received a large parcel, on which was written "The Nightingale."

"There we have a new book about this celebrated bird," said the Emperor.

But it was not a book, but a little work of art, contained in a box, an artificial nightingale, which was to sing like a natural one, and was brilliantly ornamented with diamonds, sapphires and rubies. So soon as the artificial bird

was wound up, he could sing one of the pieces that the real bird sang, and then his tail moved up and down, and shone with silver and gold. Round his neck hung a little ribbon, and on that was written, "The Emperor of China's nightingale is poor compared with that of the Emperor of Japan."

"That is capital!" said they all, and he who had brought the artificial bird immediately received the title Imperial-Head-Nightingale-Bringer.

"Now they must sing together; what a duet that will be!" cried the courtiers.

And so they had to sing together; but it did not sound very well, for the real Nightingale sang in its own way, and the artificial bird sang waltzes.

"That's not his fault," said the playmaster; "he's quite perfect, and very much in my style."

Now the artificial bird was to sing alone. It had just as much success as the real one, and then it was much handsomer to look at—it shone like bracelets and breast-pins.

Three and thirty times over did it sing the same piece, and yet was not tired. The people would gladly have heard it again, but the Emperor said that the living Nightingale ought to sing something now. But where was it? No one had noticed that it had flown away out of the open window, back to the green wood.

"But what has become of that?" asked the Emperor.

And all the courtiers abused the Nightingale, and declared that it was a very ungrateful creature.

"We have the best bird after all," said they.

And so the artificial bird had to sing again, and that was the thirty-fourth time that they listened to the same piece. For all that, they did not know it quite by heart, for it was so very difficult. And the playmaster praised the bird particularly; yes, he declared that it was better than a nightingale, not only with regard to its plumage and the many beautiful diamonds, but inside as well.

"For you see, ladies and gentlemen, and above all, your Imperial Majesty, with a real nightingale one can never calculate what is coming, but in this artificial bird everything is settled. One can explain it; one can open it and make people understand where the waltzes come from, how they go, and how one follows up another."

"Those are quite our own ideas," they all said.

And the speaker received permission to show the bird to the people on the next Sunday. The people were to hear it sing too, the Emperor commanded; and they did hear it, and were as much pleased as if they had got tipsy upon tea, for that's quite the Chinese fashion; and they all said "Oh!" and held up their forefingers and nodded. But the poor fisherman, who had heard the real Nightingale, said:

"It sounds pretty enough, and the melodies resemble each other, but there's something wanting, though I know not what!"

The real Nightingale was banished from the country and empire. The artificial bird had its place on a silken cushion close to the Emperor's bed; all the presents it had received, gold and precious stones, were ranged about it; in title it had advanced to be the High Imperial After-Dinner-Singer, and in rank to Number One on the left hand; for the Emperor considered that side the most important on which the heart is placed, and even in an Emperor the heart is on the left side; and the playmaster wrote a work of five and twenty volumes about the artificial bird: it was very learned and very long, full of the most difficult Chinese words; but yet all the people declared that they had read it and understood it, for fear of being considered stupid and having their bodies trampled on.

So a whole year went by. The Emperor, the Court, and all the other Chinese knew every little twitter in the artificial bird's song by heart. But just for that reason it pleased them best—they could sing with it themselves, and they did so. The street boys sang,

"Tsi-tsi-tsi-glug-glug!"

And the Emperor himself sang it too. Yes, that was certainly famous.

But, one evening when the artificial bird was singing its best, and the Emperor lay in bed listening to it, something inside the bird said, "Whizz!" Something cracked. "Whir-r-r!" All the wheels ran round and then the music stopped.

The Emperor immediately sprang out of bed, and caused his body physician to be called; but what could *he* do? Then they sent for a watchmaker, and after a good deal of talking and investigation, the bird was put into something like order; but the watchmaker said that the bird must be carefully treated, for the barrels were worn, and it would be impossible to put new ones in, in such a manner that the music would go. There was great lamentation; only once in the year was it permitted to let the bird sing, and that was almost too much. But then the play-master made a little speech, full of heavy words, and said this was just as good as before—and so of course it was as good as before.

Now five years had gone by and a real grief came upon the whole nation. The Chinese were really fond of their Emperor, and now he was ill, and could not, it was said, live much longer. Already a new Emperor had been chosen, and the people stood out in the streets and asked the cavalier how the Emperor did.

"P!" said he, and shook his head.

Cold and pale lay the Emperor in the great gorgeous bed; the whole court thought him dead, and each ran to pay homage to the new ruler. The chamberlain ran out to talk it over and the ladies' maids had a great coffee party. All about, in all the halls and passages, cloth had been laid down so that no footstep could be heard, and therefore it was quiet there, quite quiet. But the Emperor was not dead yet; stiff and pale he lay on the gorgeous bed with the long velvet curtains and the heavy gold tassels; high up, a window stood open, and the moon shone in upon the Emperor and the artificial bird.

The poor Emperor could scarcely breathe; it was just as if something lay upon his chest, and then he saw that it was Death who sat upon his chest, and had put on his golden crown, and held in one hand the Emperor's sword, and in the other his beautiful banner. And all around, from among the folds of the splendid velvet curtains, strange heads peered forth; a few very ugly, the rest quite lively and mild. These were all the Emperor's bad and good deeds, that stood before him now that Death sat upon his heart.

"Do you remember this?" whispered one to the other. "Do you remember that?" and then they told him so much that the perspiration ran from his forehead.

"I did not know that!" said the Emperor. "Music! Music! The great Chinese drum!" he cried, "so that I need not hear all they say!"

And they continued speaking, and Death nodded like a Chinaman to all they said.

"Music! Music!" cried the Emperor. "You little precious golden bird, sing, sing! I have given you gold and costly presents; I have even hung my golden slipper around your neck—sing now, sing!"

But the bird stood still; no one was there to wind him up, and he could not sing without that; but Death continued to stare at the Emperor with his great hollow eyes, and it was quite fearfully quiet.

Then there sounded from the window, suddenly, the most lovely song. It was the little live Nightingale, that sat outside on a spray. It had heard of the Emperor's sad plight, and had come to sing to him of comfort and hope. As it sang the spectres grew paler and paler; the blood ran

quicker and more quickly through the Emperor's weak limbs; and even Death listened, and said:

"Go on, little Nightingale, go on!"

"But will you give me that splendid golden sword? Will you give me that rich banner? Will you give me the Emperor's crown?"

And Death gave up each of these treasures for a song. And the Nightingale sang on and on; and it sang of the quiet churchyard where the white roses grow, where the elder blossoms smell sweet, and where the fresh grass is moistened by the tears of survivors. Then Death felt a longing to see his garden, and floated out of the window in the form of a cold white mist.

"Thanks! Thanks!" said the Emperor. "You heavenly little bird! I know you well. I banished you from my country and empire, and yet you have charmed away the evil faces from my couch, and banished Death from my heart! How can I reward you?"

"You have rewarded me!" replied the Nightingale. "I have drawn tears from your eyes, when I sang the first time—I shall never forget that. Those are the jewels that rejoice a singer's heart. But now sleep, and grow fresh and strong again. I will sing you something."

And it sang, and the Emperor fell into a sweet slumber. Ah! how mild and refreshing that sleep was! The sun shone upon him through the windows, when he awoke refreshed and restored; not one of his servants had yet returned, for they all thought he was dead; only the Nightingale still sat beside him and sang.

"You must always stay with me," said the Emperor. "You shall sing as you please; and I'll break the artificial bird into a thousand pieces."

"Not so," replied the Nightingale. "It did well as long

as it could: keep it as you have done till now. I cannot build my nest in the palace to dwell in it, but let me come when I feel the wish; then I will sit in the evening on the spray yonder by the window, and sing you something, so that you may be glad and thoughtful at once. I will sing of those who are happy and of those who suffer. I will sing of good and of evil that remains hidden round about you. The little singing bird flies far around, to the poor fisherman, to the peasant's roof, to every one who dwells far away from your Court. I love your heart more than your crown, and yet the crown has an air of sanctity about it. I will come and sing to you—but one thing you must promise me."

"Everything!" said the Emperor; and he stood there in his imperial robes, which he had put on himself, and pressed the sword which was heavy with gold to his heart.

"One thing I beg of you: tell no one that you have a little bird who tells you everything. Then it will all go better."

And the Nightingale flew away.

The servants came in to look at their dead Emperor, and—yes, there he stood, and the Emperor said, "Good morning!"

The Waterbeetle

HILAIRE BELLOC

The waterbeetle here shall teach
A sermon far beyond your reach:
He flabbergasts the Human Race
By gliding on the water's face
With ease, celerity and grace;
But if he ever stopped to think
Of how he did it, he would sink.

The Cat and the Dog and the Little Red Hen

IRISH FOLK-TALE

ONCE a cat and a dog and a little red hen set up house together. They agreed to share the work, but when the time came to sow the wheat-field, the cat stretched herself out in front of the fire and said she felt ill, thinking to herself:

"No one can tell how I feel, and by the time I get up from this warm spot, the wheat will have been sown."

The dog said he would come to the wheat-field soon, and then he lay in the sun and went to sleep and forgot all about it except when he turned over once and said to himself:

"I wonder how they're getting on in the wheat-field. It ought to be almost finished by now."

The little red hen went out to the wheat-field carrying the bag of seed, and she waited and waited for a long time, until the sun was high in the sky.

"What can have happened to the cat, and what can have happened to the dog? Well, well, well, there's only one thing to do: I'll do it myself," said the little red hen.

So she planted the wheat-field and went home in the evening tired out. There the cat and the dog were waiting for their supper. The little red hen was dead tired but she cooked their supper and they all lay down to sleep.

Time went on and the wheat grew big and tall, and the grain ripened on top of it, and was cut and stacked and ready to be ground into flour. The little red hen got out the quern-stone and placed it on the kitchen floor and said:

"Tomorrow we must grind the wheat to make flour."

In the morning the cat was nowhere to be found. She had gone out early to hunt mice and birds, saying to herself:

"No one will be able to find me, I climb so high and run so fast. By the time I get home in the evening, the wheat will all have been ground."

The dog said that he had promised the farmer who had cut the wheat for them, that he would help in rounding up his sheep for market, and he went out early and ran along under the hedge until he found a quiet place for a sleep. There he lay down, saying to himself:

"I'll just take a little rest before helping with the quern. After all, the stone can only be turned by one person at a time."

Then he forgot all about it except when he turned over once and said to himself:

"I wonder if they have done much grinding by now. I needn't go until it's two-thirds done."

The little red hen began to grind the wheat, turning the quern-stone round and round by its handle, and very tiring indeed she found it. When she had finished one-third she waited for a while to see if the cat would come and help her. When she did not, the little red hen worked on until it was two-thirds done and then she waited for a while to see if the dog would come.

"What can have happened to them? Why haven't they

come to help me grind the wheat? Well, well, well, there's only one thing to do: I'll do it myself," said the little red hen.

And she turned and turned the quern-stone until all the wheat was ground into flour. Just as she had finished, the cat and the dog appeared and said:

"Oh, you good little red hen! You have finished the grinding just in time to get us our supper."

The little red hen said nothing but cooked supper for all of them, and they all lay down to sleep.

The next day the little red hen heated up the oven and said:

"Today we must make lots of bread out of our new flour. We'll make dozens and dozens of wheat-cakes that can be stored away for the winter."

While her back was turned, the cat slipped out of the house and went down to the river to look for a fish for her breakfast, thinking to herself:

"The hen is afraid of the water, and the dog is too stupid to know where to look for me, and by the time I get back, all the baking will have been done."

The dog said he would go out and look for the cat, who must be taught to do her share of the work like everyone else, and he went off to a wood five miles away where he knew the cat sometimes went hunting. There he found that the run had tired him and he lay down to rest himself, saying:

"I'll get back in time to stoke the fire. After all, I'm not a good baker, and that fire was good for a few hours at least."

Then he forgot all about it, except when he turned over once and said to himself:

"I must run back to the house soon and see how things

are going there, because it's very important to have lots of wheat-cakes stored for the winter."

The little red hen made wheat-cakes and baked them in the pot-oven one by one, until she was exhausted. The sun had gone up one side of the sky and down the other, and in the middle of the afternoon when the baking was half-done, she stopped for a short time to rest, standing at the door to see if the dog or the cat were coming.

"That's very strange. I wonder why they haven't come to help me bake the bread. Well, well, well, it's hard, hot work but there's only one thing to be done: I'll do it myself," said the little red hen.

And she turned back wearily to the fire and went on with the baking, until she had made a great pile of wheat-cakes, enough to last the whole winter through. When she had finished, she locked the door, cooked her supper and went to sit quietly by the fire.

Soon afterwards, the dog and the cat came home and they were astonished when they found the door shut against them.

"Open up, open up, you good little hen!" they called out. "Let us in and cook us some supper!"

Without stirring from the fire, the little red hen asked:

"And why would I do that?"

"Because we agreed to share and share alike, because you always cook our supper, because you are such a good, generous, kind-hearted, hard-working person."

"That's as may be, but I'm tired now and I've had my supper, and I'm not opening the door to anyone. First I sowed the wheat and then I ground it, and today I've spent the whole day making it into wheat-cakes for the winter, and neither of you came to help me do all that work."

"But the wheat-cakes!" they cried out together. "You have so many of them! What will you do with all those wheat-cakes?"

"I'll eat them myself!" said the little red hen.

So the dog and the cat had to find another lodging.

Retold by EILÍS DILLON

The King of the Cats

PADRAIC COLUM

THE King of the Cats stood up. He was a grand creature. His body was brown and striped across as if one had burned on wood with a hot poker. Like all the race of the Royal Cats of the Isle of Man he was without a tail. But he had extraordinarily fine whiskers. They went each side of his face to the length of a dinner dish. He had such eyes that when he turned one of them upward the bird that was flying across dropped from the sky. And when he turned the other one down he could make a hole in the floor.

He lived in the Isle of Man. Once he had been King of the Cats of Ireland and Britain, of Norway and Denmark, and the whole Northern and Western World. But after the Norsemen won in the wars the Cats of Norway and Britain swore by Thor and Odin that they would give him no more allegiance. So for a hundred years and a day he had got allegiance only from the Cats of the Western World; that is from Ireland and the Islands beyond.

The tribute he received was still worth having. In May he was sent a boatful of herring. In August he was let have two boatfuls of mackerel. In November he was given five barrels of preserved mice. At other seasons he had for his tribute one out of every hundred birds that flew across the

Island on their way to Ireland—tomtits, pee-wits, linnets, siskins, starlings, martins, wrens, and tender young barn owls. He was also sent the following as marks of allegiance and respect: a salmon to show his dominion over the rivers; the skin of a marten to show his dominion in the woods; a live cricket to show his dominion in the houses of men; the horn of a cow, to show his right to a portion of the milk produced in the Western World.

But the tribute from the Western World became smaller and smaller. One year the boat did not come with the herring. Mackerel was sent to him afterwards but he knew it was sent to him because so much was being taken out of the sea that the farmermen were ploughing their mackerel catches into the land to make their crops grow. Then a year came when he got neither the salmon nor the marten skin, neither the live cricket nor the cow's horn. Then he got righteously and royally indignant. He stood up on his four paws on the floor of his palace, and declared to his wife that he himself was going to Ireland to know what prevented the sending of his lawful tribute to him. He called for his Prime Minister then and said,

"Prepare for Us our Speech from the Throne."

The Prime Minister went to the Parliament House and wrote down "Oyez, Oyez, Oyez!" But he could not remember any more of the ancient language in which the speeches from the Throne were always written. He went home and hanged himself with a measure of tape and his wife buried the body under the hearthstone.

"Speech or no speech," said the King of the Cats, "I'm going to pay a royal visit to my subjects in Ireland."

He went to the top of the cliff and he made a spring. He landed on the deck of a ship that was bringing the King of Norway's daughter to be married to the King of Scotland's son. The ship nearly sank with the crash of his body on it. He ran up the sails and placed himself on the mast of the ship. There he gathered his feet together and made another spring. This time he landed on a boat that was bringing oak-timber to build a King's Palace in London. He stood where the timber was highest and made another spring. This time he landed on the Giant's Causeway that runs from Ireland out into the sea. He picked his steps from boulder to boulder, and then walked royally and resolutely on the ground of Ireland. A man was riding on horseback with a woman seated on the saddle behind him. The King of the Cats waited until they came up.

"My good man," said he very grandly, "when you go back to your house tell the ash-covered cat in the corner that the King of the Cats has come to Ireland to see him."

His manner was so grand that the man took off his hat and the woman made a curtsey. Then the King of the Cats sprang into the branch of a tree of the forest and slept till it was past the midday heat.

I nearly forgot to tell you that as he slept on the branch his whiskers stood around his face the breadth of a dinner dish either way.

The King of the Cats waited on the branch of the tree until the moon was in the sky like a roast duck on a dish of gold, and still neither retainer, vassal nor subject came to do him service. He was vexed, I tell you, at the want of respect shown him.

This was the reason why none of his subjects came to him for such a long time: The man and woman he had spoken to went into their house and did not say a word about the King of the Cats until they had eaten their supper. Then when the man had smoked his second pipe he said to the woman:

"That was a wonderful thing that happened to us today. A cat to walk up to two Christians and say to them, 'Tell the ashy pet in your chimney corner at home that the King of the Cats has come to see him.' "

No sooner were the words said than the lean, grey, ash-covered cat that lay on the hearthstone sprang on the back of the man's chair.

"I will say this," said the man; "it's a bad time when two Christians like ourselves are stopped on their way back from the market and ordered—ordered, no less—to give a message to one's own cat lying on one's own hearthstone."

"By my fur and claws, you're a long time coming to his message," said the cat on the back of the chair; "what was it, anyway?"

"The King of the Cats has come to Ireland to see you," said the man, very much surprised.

"It's a wonder you told it at all," said the cat, going to the door. "And where did you see His Majesty?"

"You shouldn't have spoken," said the man's wife.

"And how did I know a cat could understand?" said the man.

"When you have done talking among yourselves," said the cat, "would you tell me where you met His Majesty?"

"Nothing will I tell you," said the man, "until I hear your own name from you."

"My name," said the cat, "is Quick-to-Grab, and well you should know it."

"Not a word will we tell you," said the woman, "until we hear what the King of the Cats is doing in Ireland. Is he bringing wars and rebellions into the country?"

"Wars and rebellions—no, ma'am," said Quick-to-Grab, "but deliverance from oppression. Why are the cats of the country lean and lazy and covered with ashes? It is because the cat that goes outside the house in the sunlight, to hunt or to play, is made to suffer with the loss of an eye."

"And who makes them suffer with the loss of an eye?" said the woman.

"One whose reign is nearly over now," said Quick-to-Grab. "But tell me where you saw His Majesty?"

"No," said the man.

"No," said the woman, "for we don't like your impertinence. Back with you to the hearthstone, and watch the mouse-hole for us."

Quick-to-Grab walked straight out of the door.

"May no prosperity come to this house," said he, "for denying me when I asked where the King of the Cats was pleased to speak to you."

But he put his ear to the door when he went outside and he heard the woman say:

"The horse will tell that we saw the King of the Cats a mile this side of the Giant's Causeway."

(That was a mistake. The horse could not have told it at all, because horses never know the language that is spoken in houses—only cats know it fully and dogs know a little of it.)

Quick-to-Grab now knew where the King of the Cats might be found. He went creeping by hedges, loping across fields, bounding through woods, until he came under the branch in the forest where the King of the Cats rested, his whiskers standing round his face the breadth of a dinner dish.

When he came under the branch Quick-to-Grab mewed a little in Egyptian, which is the ceremonial language of the cats. The King of the Cats came to the end of the branch.

"Who are you, vassal?" said he in Phoenician.

"A humble retainer of my lord," said Quick-to-Grab in High-Pictish (this is a language very suitable to cats but it is only their historians who now use it.)

They continued their conversation in Irish.

"What sign shall I show the others that will make them know you are the King of the Cats?" said Quick-to-Grab.

The King of the Cats chased up the tree and pulled down heavy branches. "There is a sign of my royal prowess," said he.

"It's a good sign," said Quick-to-Grab.

They were about to talk again when Quick-to-Grab put down his tail and ran up another tree greatly frightened.

"What ails you?" said the King of the Cats. "Can you not stay while you're speaking to your lord and master?"

"Old-fellow Badger is coming this way," said Quick-to-Grab, "and when he puts his teeth in one he never lets go."

Without saying a word the King of the Cats jumped down from the tree. Old-fellow Badger was coming through the glade. When he saw the King of the Cats crouching there he stopped and bared his terrible teeth. The King of the Cats bent himself to spring. Then Old-fellow Badger turned round and went lumbering back.

"Oh, by my claws and fur," said Quick-to-Grab, "you are the real King of the Cats. Let me be your Councillor. Let me advise your Majesty in the times that will be so difficult for your subjects and yourself. Know that the cats of Ireland are impoverished and oppressed. They are under a terrible tyranny."

"Who oppresses my vassals, retainers and subjects?" said the King of the Cats.

"The Eagle-Emperor. He has made a law that no cat

may leave a man's house as long as the birds (he makes an exception in the case of owls) have any business abroad."

"I will tear him to pieces," said the King of the Cats. "How can I reach him?"

"No cat has thought of reaching him," said Quick-to-Grab, "they only think of keeping out of his way. Now let me advise your Majesty. None of our enemies must know that you have come into this country. You must appear as a common cat."

"What, me?" said the King of the Cats.

"Yes, your Majesty, for the sake of the deliverance of your subjects you will have to appear as a common cat."

"And be submissive and eat scraps?"

"That will be only in the daytime," said Quick-to-Grab, "in the night-time you will have your court and your feasts."

"At least, let the place I stay in be no hovel," said the King of the Cats. "I shall refuse to go into a house where there are washing days—damp clothes before a fire and all that."

"I shall use my best diplomacy to safeguard your comfort and dignity," said Quick-to-Grab. "Please invest me as your Prime Minister."

The King of the Cats invested Quick-to-Grab by biting the fur round his neck. Then the King and his Prime Minister parted. The King of the Cats took up quarters for a day or two in a round tower. Quick-to-Grab made a journey through the countryside. He went into every house and whispered a word to every cat that was there, and whether the cat was watching a mouse-hole, or chasing crickets, or playing with kittens, when he or she heard that word they sat up and considered.

Quick-to-Grab, in consultation with the Seven Elders of

the Cat-Kin, decided that the Blacksmith's forge would be a fit residence for the King of the Cats. It was clean and commodious. But the best reason of all for his going there was this: people and beasts from all parts came into the forge and the King of the Cats might learn from their discussions where the Eagle-Emperor was and how he might be destroyed.

His Majesty found that the Forge was not a bad residence for a King living unbeknownst. It was dry and warm. He liked the look of the flames that mounted up with the blowing of the bellows. He used to sit on a heap of old saddles on the floor and watch the horses being shod or waiting to be shod. He listened to the talk of the men. The people in the Forge treated him respectfully and often referred to his size, his appearance and his fine manners.

Every night he went out to a feast that the cats had prepared for him. Quick-to-Grab always walked back to the Forge with him to give a Prime Minister's advice. He warned His Majesty not to let the human beings know that he understood and could converse in their language—(all cats know men's language but men do not know that the cats know). He told him not to be too haughty (as a King might be inclined to be) to any creature in the Forge.

The King of the Cats took this advice. He used even to twitch his ears as a mark of respect to Mahon, the hound whose kennel was just outside the Forge, and to the hounds that Mahon had to visit him. He even made advances to the Cock who walked up and down outside.

This Cock made himself very annoying to the King of the Cats. He used to strut up and down saying to himself over and over again:

"I'm Cock-o'-the-Walk! I'm Cock-o'-the-Walk!"

Sometimes he would come into the Forge and say it to

the horses. The King of the Cats wondered how the human beings could put up with a creature who was so stupid and vain. He had a red comb that fell over one eye. He had purple feathers on his tail. He had great spurs on his heels. He used to put his head on one side and yawn when the King of the Cats appeared.

Cock-o'-the-Walk used to come into the Forge at night and sleep on the bellows. And when the King of the Cats came back from the feasts he used to waken up and say to himself:

"I'm Cock-o'-the Walk, I'm Cock-o'-the-Walk. The Cats are not a respectable people."

One noonday there were men in the Forge. They were talking to the Smith. Said one:

"Could you tell us, Smith, where iron came from?"

The King of the Cats knew but he said nothing. Cock-o'-the-Walk came to the door and held his head as if he were listening.

"I can't tell where iron came from," said the Smith, "but if that Cock could talk he could tell you. The world knows that the Cock is the wisest and the most ancient of creatures."

"I'm Cock-o'-the-Walk," said the Cock to a rusty ass's shoe.

"Yes, the Cock is a wonderful creature," said the man who had asked the question.

"Not wonderful at all," said the King of the Cats, "and if you had asked me I could have told you where iron came from."

"And where did iron come from?" said the Smith.

"From the Mountains of the Moon," said the King of the Cats.

The men in the Forge put their hands on their knees and

looked down at him. Mahon the hound came into the Forge with other hounds at his tail, and seeing the men looking at the King of the Cats, Mahon put his nose to him. Cock-o'-the-Walk flapped his wings insolently. The King of the Cats struck at the red hanging comb with his paw. The Cock flew up in the air. The King of the Cats sprang out of the window, and as he did, Mahon and the other hounds sprang after him.

By the magic powers they possessed it was made known to all the cats in the country that their King was being pursued by the hounds. Then on every hearthstone a cat howled. Cats sprang to the doors, overturning cradles upon children. They stood upon the thresholds and they all made the same curse:

"That ye may break your backs, that ye may break your backs before ye catch the King of the Cats."

When he heard the howls of his vassals, retainers and subjects, the King of the Cats turned over on his back and clawed at the first hound that came after him. He stood up then. So firmly did he set himself on his four legs that those that dashed at him did not overthrow him. He humped up his body and lifted his fore-paws. The hounds held back. A horn sounded and that gave them an excuse to get away from the claws and the teeth, the power and the animosity of the King of the Cats.

Then, though it might cost each and every one of them the loss of an eye, the cats that had sight of him came running up. "We will go with you, my lord, we will help you, my lord," they all cried together.

"Go back to the hearthstones," said the King of the Cats. "Go back and be civil and quiet again in the houses. You will hear of my deeds. I go to find the tracks of our enemy, the Eagle-Emperor."

When they heard that announcement the cats lamented, and the noise of their lamentation was so dreadful that horses broke their harnesses where they were yoked; men and women lost the colour of their faces thinking some dreadful visitation was coming on the land; every bag of oats and rye turned five times to the right and five times to the left with the fright it got; dishes were broken, knives were hurled round, and the King's Castle was shaken to the bottom stone.

"It is not the time to seek the tracks of the Eagle-Emperor," said Quick-to-Grab. "Stay for a while longer in men's houses."

"Never," said the King of the Cats. "Never will I stay by the hearthstone and submit to be abused by cocks and hounds and men. I will range the world openly now and seek out the enemy of the Cat-Kind, the Eagle-Emperor."

Without once turning his back he went towards the wood that was filled with his enemies, the birds. The cats, when they saw their petitions were no use, went everyone back to the house where he or she stayed. Each one sat before a mouse-hole and pretended to be watching. But though mice stirred all round them the cats of Ireland never turned a head that night.

It was the wren, the smallest of birds, that saw him and knew him for the King of the Cats. The wren flew through the wood to summon the Hawk-Clan. But it was towards sunset now and the hawks had taken up their stations at the edge of the wood to watch that they might pick up the farmer's chickens. They wouldn't turn an eye when the wren told them that a cat was in the wood during the time forbidden to cats to be outside the houses of men.

"It is the King of the Cats," said the wren.

None of the hawks lifted a wing. They were waiting for

the chickens that would stray about the moment after sunset.

But if the wren couldn't rouse the Hawk-Clan she was able to rouse the other bird-tribes.

"A cat, a cat, on your lives a cat," she called out as she flew through the wood.

The rooks that were going home now rose above the trees, cawing threats. The blackbirds, thrushes and jays screamed as they flew before the King of the Cats. The woodpeckers, hedge-sparrows, tom-tits, robins and linnets chattered as they flew behind him. Sometimes the young rooks made a great show of attacking him. They flew down from the flock. "He is here, here, here," they cawed and flew up again. The rooks kept telling themselves and the other birds in the wood what they were going to do with the King of the Cats. But a single raven did more against him than the thousand rooks that made so much noise. This raven was in a hole in the tree. She struck the King of the Cats on the head with her beak as he went past.

The King of the Cats was annoyed by the uproar the birds were making and he was angered by the raven's stroke, but he did not want to enter into a battle with the birds. He was on his way to the house of the Hag of the Wood who was then known as the Hag of the Ashes. I'll have to tell you how the King of the Cats had heard of her and how he knew where her house was in the wood.

Quick-to-Grab had said to the King of the Cats:

"If ever you need the counsel of a human being, go to no one else but the Hag of the Ashes who was once called the Hag of the Wood. In the very centre of the wood four ash trees are drawn together at the tops, wattles are woven around these ash trees, and in the little house made in this way the Hag of the Ashes lives, with no one near her since her nine daughters went away, but her goat that is her only friend."

The King of the Cats was now in the centre of the wood. He saw four ash trees drawn together at the tops and he jumped to them.

Now the Hag of the Ashes had a bad neighbour. This was a crane that had built her nest across the roof of the little house. The nest prevented the smoke from coming out at the top and the house below was filled with it. The Hag could hardly keep alive on account of the smoke and she could neither take away the nest nor banish the bird.

The crane was there when the King of the Cats sprang on the roof. She was sitting with her two legs stretched out and when the King of the Cats came down beside her she slipped away and sailed over the trees.

"Time for me to be going," said the crane. And from that day to this she never came back to the house of the Hag of the Ashes.

"Oh, thanks to you, good creature," said the Hag of the Ashes, coming out of the house. "Tear down her nest now and let the smoke rise up through the roof."

The King of the Cats tore up the sticks and wool that the crane's nest was made of, and the smoke came up through the top of the house. "Oh, thanks to you, good creature, that has destroyed the cross crane's nest. Come down on my floor now and I'll do everything that will serve you."

The King of the Cats jumped down on the floor of the Hag's house and saw the Hag of the Ashes sitting in a corner. She was a little, little woman in a grey cloak. All over the floor there were ashes in heaps, for she used to light a fire in one corner and when it was burnt out light another beside the ashes of the first. The smoke had never gone through the hole in the roof since the crane had built her nest on the top of the house. Her face was yellow with the smoke and her eyes were half closed on account of it.

"Do you know who I am, Hag of the Ashes?" said the King of the Cats when he stood on the floor.

"You are a cat, honey," said the Hag of the Ashes.

"I am the King of the Cats."

"The King of the Cats you are indeed. And it was you who let the smoke out of the top of my little house by destroying the nest the cross crane had built on it."

"It was I who did that."

"Welcome to you then, King of the Cats. And what service can the Hag of the Ashes do for you in return?"

"I would go where the Eagle-Emperor is. You must show me the way."

"By my cloak I will do that. The Eagle-Emperor lives on the top of the Hill of Horns."

"And how can I get to the top of the Hill of Horns?"

"I don't know how you can get there at all. All over the Hill is bare starvation. No four-footed thing can reach the top—no four-footed thing, I mean, but my goat that's tied to the hawthorn bush outside."

"I will ride on the back of your goat to the top of the Hill of Horns."

"No, no, good King of the Cats. I have only my goat for company and how could I bear to be parted from him?"

"Lend me your goat, and when I come back from the Hill of Horns I will plate his horns with gold and shoe his hooves with silver."

"No, no, good King of the Cats. How could I bear my goat to be away from me, and I having no other company?"

"If you do not let me ride your goat to the top of the Hill of Horns, I will leave a sign on your house that will bring the cross crane to build her nest on the top of it again."

"Then take my goat, King of the Cats, take my goat but let him come back to me soon."

"I will. Come with me now and bid him take me to the top of the Hill of Horns."

The King of the Cats marched out of the house and the Hag of the Ashes hobbled after him. The goat was lying under the hawthorn bush. He put his horns to the ground when they came up to him.

"Will you go to the Hill of Horns?" said the Hag of the Ashes.

"Indeed that I will not do," said the goat.

"Oh, the soft tops of the hedges on the way to the Hill of Horns—sweet in the mouth of a goat they should be," said the Hag of the Ashes. "But my own poor goat wants to stay here and eat the tops of the burnt-up thistles."

"Why didn't you tell me of the hedges on the way to the Hill of Horns before?" said the goat, rising to his feet. "To the Hill of Horns I'll go."

"And will you let a cat ride on your back to the Hill of Horns?"

"Indeed, I will not do that."

"Then, my poor goat, I'll not untie the rope that's round your neck, for you can't go to the Hill of Horns without this cat riding on your back."

"Let him sit on my back, then, and hold my horns, and I'll take no notice of him."

The Hag of the Ashes untied the rope that was round his neck, the King of the Cats jumped up on the goat's back and they started off on the path through the wood.

"Oh, how I'll miss my goat, until he comes back to me with gold on his horns and silver on his hooves," the Hag of the Ashes cried after them.

What should a goat do but ramble down laneways, wander across fields, stray along hedges and stay to rest under shady trees? All this the Hag's goat did. But at last he brought the King of the Cats to the foot of the Hill of Horns.

And what was the Hill of Horns like, asks my kind foster child. It was hills of stones on the top of a hill of stones. Only a goat could foot it from pebble to stone, from stone to boulder, from boulder to crag, and from crag to mountain-shoulder. It was well and not ill that the Hag's goat did. But then thunder sounded; lightning struck fire out of the stones, the wind mixed itself with the rain and the tempest pelted cat and goat. The goat stood on the mountain shoulder. The wind rushed up from the bottom and carried the companions to the top of the Hill of Horns. Down sprang the cat. But the goat stood on his hind legs to butt back at the wind. The wind caught him between the beard and the underquarters and swept him from the top and down the other side of the hill (and what happened to the Hag's goat after that I never heard). The King of the Cats put his claws into the crevices of a standing stone and held to it with great tenacity. And then, when the wind abated he looked across his shoulder, he found that he was standing beside the nest of the Eagle-Emperor.

It was a hollow edged with rocks, and round that hollow were scattered the horns of the deer and goats that the Eagle-Emperor had carried off. And in the hollow there was a calf and a hare and a salmon. The King of the Cats sprang into the Eagle-Emperor's nest. First he ate the salmon. Then he stretched himself between the hare and the calf and waited for the Eagle-Emperor.

At last he appeared. Down he came to the nest making circles in the air. He lighted on the rocky rim. The King of the Cats rose with body bent for the spring, and if the Eagle-Emperor was not astonished at his appearance it was because an Eagle can never be astonished.

A brave man would be glad if he could have seen the Eagle-Emperor as he crouched there on the rock rim of his nest. He spread down his wings till they were great strong shields. He bent down his outspread tail. He bent down his neck so that his eyes might look into the creature that faced him. And his cruel, curved, heavy beak was ready for the stroke.

But the King of the Cats sprang into the air. The Eagle lifted himself up but the Cat came down on his broad back. The Eagle-Emperor screamed his war-scream and flew off the hill. He struck at the King of the Cats with the backs of his broad wings. Then he plunged down. On the stones below he would tear his enemy with beak and claws.

It was the Cat that reached the ground. As the Eagle went to strike at him he sprang again and tore the Eagle's breast. Then the Eagle-Emperor caught the King of the Cats in his claws and flew up again, screaming his battle-scream. Drops of blood from both fell to the ground. The Eagle had not a conquerer's grip on his enemy and the King of the Cats was able to tear at him.

It happened that Curoi, King of the Munster Fairies, was marching at the head of his troop to play a game of hurling with the Fianna of Ireland, captained by Fergus, and for the hand of Ainé, the daughter of Mannanaun, the Lord of the Sea. Just when the ball was about to be thrown in the air the Eagle-Emperor and the King of the Cats were seen mixed together in their struggle. One troop took the side of the Eagle and the other took the side of the

Cat. The men of the country came up and took sides too. Then the men began to fight among themselves and some were left dead on the ground. And this went on until there were hosts of the men of Ireland fighting each other on account of the Eagle-Emperor and the King of the Cats.

The King of the Fairies and the Chief of the Fianna marched their men away to a hill top where they might watch the battle in the air and the battles on the ground.

"If this should go on," said Curoi, "our troops will join in and men and fairies will be slaughtered. We must end the combat in the air."

Saying this he took up the hurling-ball and flung it at the Cat and Eagle. Both came down on the ground. The Cat was about to spring, the Eagle was about to pounce, when Curoi darted between them and struck both with his spear. Eagle and Cat became figures of stone. And there they are now, a Stone Eagle with his wings outspread and a Stone Cat with his teeth bared and his paws raised. And the Eagle-Emperor and the King of the Cats will remain like that until Curoi strikes them again with his fairy spear.

When the Cat and the Eagle were turned into stone the men of the country wondered for a while and then they went away. And the Fairies of Munster and the Fianna of Ireland played the hurling match for the hand of Ainé the daughter of Mannanaun, who is Lord of the Sea, and what the result of that hurling match was is told in another book.

And that ends my history of the coming into Ireland of the King of the Cats.

From THE KING OF IRELAND'S SON

Mr. Mistoffelees

T. S. ELIOT

You ought to know Mr. Mistoffelees!
The Original Conjuring Cat—
(There can be no doubt about that).
Please listen to me and don't scoff. All his
Inventions are off his own bat.
There's no such cat in the metropolis;
He holds all the patent monopolies
For performing surprising illusions
And creating eccentric confusions.
  At prestidigitation
    And at legerdemain
  He'll defy examination
    And deceive you again.
The greatest magicians have something to learn
From Mr. Mistoffelees' Conjuring Turn.
Presto!
  Away we go!
    And we all say: OH!
      Well I never!
      Was there ever
      A Cat so clever
        As Magical Mr. Mistoffelees!

He is quiet and small, he is black

From his ears to the tip of his tail;
He can creep through the tiniest crack,
He can walk on the narrowest rail.
He can pick any card from a pack,
He is equally cunning with dice;
He is always deceiving you into believing
That he's only hunting for mice.
  He can play any trick with a cork
    Or a spoon and a bit of fish-paste;
  If you look for a knife or a fork
    And you think it is merely misplaced—
You have seen it one moment, and then it is *gawn*!
But you'll find it next week lying out on the lawn.
  And we all say: OH!
    Well I never!
    Was there ever
    A Cat so clever
      As Magical Mr. Mistoffelees!

His manner is vague and aloof,
You would think there was nobody shyer—
But his voice has been heard on the roof
When he was curled up by the fire.
And he's sometimes been heard by the fire
When he was about on the roof—
(At least we all *heard* that somebody purred)
Which is incontestable proof
  Of his singular magical powers:
    And I have known the family to call
  Him in from the garden for hours,
    While he was asleep in the hall.
And not so long ago this phenomenal Cat
Produced *seven kittens* right out of a hat!

And we all said: OH!
  Well I never!
  Did you ever
  Know a Cat so clever
    As Magical Mr. Mistoffelees!

From OLD POSSUM'S BOOK
OF PRACTICAL CATS

Timothy the Tortoise

GILBERT WHITE

The Rev. Gilbert White was Curate of Selborne in Hampshire, where his family had lived for hundreds of years. He owned an estate with large gardens, and loved to entertain his friends and relations there, and to visit them from time to time. His great book is The Natural History of Selborne, *some of it a straight account of the plants, animals and birds which he saw around him, some of it in the form of letters to his friends.*

The tortoise called Timothy belonged to Mrs. Rebecca Snooke, a widow, who was Gilbert White's aunt. Her husband had bought it in Chichester from a sailor, for half a crown, and brought it back to his house at Ringmer in Sussex. Forty years later the tortoise was still there, and when Gilbert White visited his aunt, then an old lady of seventy-six, he began to watch Timothy and make notes of how he spent his time. The tortoise liked Mrs. Snooke and came to her when she appeared in the garden, knowing that she would have some kidney-beans and cucumber for him.

When the old lady died, Gilbert White took the tortoise to Selborne, eighty miles in a post-chaise, and established him in the garden, under the special care of the gardener, Thomas Hoar. It was winter when the move was made and Timothy had to be dug out of his hibernating spot. He showed his annoyance by hissing.

Gilbert White studied him for a long time, noting what he liked to eat, putting him into a tub of water to see if he could swim, which he could not, shouting at him through a speaking trumpet, which he ignored, weighing him and generally annoying poor Timothy, whose greatest attribute seems to me to have been his patience. He even endured being called an "abject reptile".

April 12, 1772
To the Hon. Daines Barrington

DEAR Sir,

While I was in Sussex last autumn my residence was at the village near Lewes, from whence I had formerly the pleasure of writing to you. On the first of November I remarked that the old tortoise, formerly mentioned, began first to dig the ground in order to the forming of its hybernaculum, which it had fixed on just beside a great tuft of hepaticas. It scrapes out the ground with its forefeet, and throws it up over its back with its hind; but the motion of its legs is ridiculously slow, little exceeding the hour-hand of a clock; and suitable to the composure of an animal said to be a whole month in performing one feat of copulation. Nothing can be more assiduous than this creature night and day in scooping the earth, and forcing its great body into the cavity; but, as the noons of that season proved unusually warm and sunny, it was continually interrupted, and called forth by the heat in the middle of the day; and though I continued there till the thirteenth of November, yet the work remained unfinished. Harsher weather, and frosty mornings, would have quickened its operations. No part of its behaviour ever struck me more than the extreme timidity it always expresses with regard to rain; for though it has a shell that would secure it against the wheel of a loaded cart, yet does it discover as much solicitude about rain as a lady dressed in all her best attire, shuffling away on the first sprinklings, and running its head up in a corner. If attended to, it becomes an excellent weather-glass; for as sure as it walks elate, and as it were on tiptoe, feeding with great earnestness in a morning, so sure will it rain before night. It is totally a diurnal animal, and never pretends to stir after it becomes dark. The tortoise, like other reptiles, has an arbitrary stomach as well as lungs; and can refrain from eating as well as breathing for a great part of the year. When first awakened it eats nothing; nor again in the autumn before it retires: through the height of the summer it feeds voraciously, devouring all the food that comes in its way. I was much taken with its sagacity in discerning those that do it kind offices: for as soon as the good old lady comes in sight who has waited on it for more than thirty years, it hobbles towards its benefactress with awkward alacrity; but remains inattentive to strangers. Thus not only 'the ox knoweth his owner, and the ass his master's crib,' but the most abject reptile and torpid of beings distinguishes the hand that feeds it, and is touched with the feelings of gratitude!

I am, etc. etc.

P.S. In about three days after I left Sussex the tortoise retired into the ground under the hepatica.

Further Particulars respecting the Old Family Tortoise

GILBERT WHITE

BECAUSE we call this creature an abject reptile, we are too apt to undervalue his abilities, and depreciate his powers of instinct. Yet he is, as Mr. Pope says of his lord,

"....much too wise to walk into a well:"

and has so much discernment as not to fall down an haha; but to stop and withdraw from the brink with the readiest precaution.

Though he loves warm weather he avoids the hot sun; because his thick shell, when once heated, would, as the poet says of solid armour—"scald with safety." He therefore spends the more sultry hours under the umbrella of a huge cabbage-leaf, or amidst the waving forests of an asparagus-bed.

But as he avoids heat in the summer, so, in the decline of the year, he improves the faint autumnal beams, by getting within the reflection of a fruit wall: and, though he has never read that planes inclining to the horizon receive a greater share of warmth, he inclines his shell, by tilting it against the wall, to collect and admit every feeble ray.

Pitiable seems the condition of this poor embarrassed reptile: to be cased in a suit of ponderous armour, which he cannot lay aside; to be imprisoned, as it were, within his own shell, must preclude, we should suppose, all activity and disposition for enterprise. Yet there is a season of the year (usually the beginning of June) when his exertions are remarkable. He then walks on tiptoe, and is stirring by five in the morning; and, traversing the garden, examines every wicket and interstice in the fences, through which he will escape if possible: and often has eluded the care of the gardener, and wandered to some distant field. The motives that impel him to undertake these rambles seem to be of the amorous kind: his fancy then becomes intent on sexual attachments, which transport him beyond his usual gravity, and induce him to forget for a time his ordinary solemn deportment.

From THE NATURAL HISTORY OF SELBORNE

Acknowledgements

Ernest Benn Ltd, London, for permission to include *The Psammead* from FIVE CHILDREN AND IT by E. Nesbit.

Mrs George Bambridge, the Macmillan Co. of London and Basingstoke and the Macmillan Co. of Canada Ltd, and Doubleday & Company Inc., New York, for permission to include *Mowgli's Brothers* from THE JUNGLE BOOK by Rudyard Kipling.

The Society of Authors as the literary representatives of the Estate of John Masefield, and Macmillan Publishing Co. Inc. (copyright 1927 and renewed 1955 by John Masefield) for *Rollicum Bitem the Fox* from THE MIDNIGHT FOX by John Masefield.

Mr Robert Farren for permission to include his poem THE PETS.

Oxford University Press, London, for permission to include an extract from KPO THE LEOPARD by René Guillot.

The Loeb Classical Library, William Heinemann Ltd, London, and Harvard University Press, Cambridge, Mass., for permission to include extracts from PLINY: NATURAL HISTORY, translated by H. Rackham.

David Higham Associates and Jonathan Cape Ltd, London, for permission to include *The Lion*, *Of Parrots* and *Of Crabs* from THE BOOK OF BEASTS by T. H. White.

Penguin Books Ltd, for *Odysseus and Argus* from THE ODYSSEY by Homer, translated by E. V. Rieu, and for *An Intelligent Monkey* from THE BOOK OF THE COURTIER by Baldassare Castiglione, translated by George Bull.

Gerald Duckworth, London, and Alfred A. Knopf Inc., New York, for permission to include *The Yak* from A BAD CHILD'S BOOK OF BEASTS by Hilaire Belloc.

George G. Harrap & Company Ltd, London, and Macmillan Publishing Co. Inc., for permission to include *The King of the Cats* from THE KING OF IRELAND'S SON by Padraic Colum; copyright 1916 by Macmillan Publishing Co. Inc., renewed 1944 by Padraic Colum.

Faber & Faber Ltd, London, and Harcourt, Brace Jovanovitch Inc., New York, for permission to include *Mr Mistoffelees* from OLD POSSUM'S BOOK OF PRACTICAL CATS by T. S. Eliot (Copyright 1939 by Esme Valerie Eliot).